# "I How Could He . . .!?"

An ordinary journey with
an extraordinary God

CAROL SPURGEON

ISBN 978-1-68197-555-9 (Paperback)
ISBN 978-1-68197-556-6 (Digital)

Christian Faith Publishing, Inc.
296 Chestnut Street
Meadville, PA 16335
www.christianfaithpublishing.com

Printed in the United States of America

# Contents

**PART II**

9-23-2018

To Charlie, family,
 To Memories
 To God's blessings on Each

 Forever,
   Carol Spurgeon

## "HOW COULD HE . . .!?"

It could be—"Once upon a time—
  there was a little girl—
    born in a brown asphalt rented house.
  She was quite ordinary.
  Her family had no claim to fame.
God saw the little girl.
He saw her looking at the moon feeling small and awestruck.
  He saw her tears of repentance.
Later, He saw her tears of commitment and surrender.
  He saw her crying on the steps holding the journal wrinkled
  with tears."

        ……"How could He…!?"

*Carol Jean Davolt near the brown asphalt house*

*Mother, Alliene Clouse Davolt and Carol*

# Chapter 1

## BROWN ASPHALT HOUSE

My sleepy four-year-old eyes sought a squinting revenge against the sudden brightness as the pull chain light illuminated the tiny room used as kitchen.

"Get the broom!" Mother yelled. She sounded urgent.

With the light coming on, the small back porch-turned-kitchen suddenly contrasted with the dark night hour. We were returning from church to the lightless house, finding more occupants—the nocturnal gathering of cockroaches. Their own congregation chose the cool and dark environment of the concrete kitchen floor, once a porch. These uninvited guests created a lively scramble. It seemed to me that the floor was alive. Not only was it alive, it was black and moving!

"Out the back door," Mother continued as she swept away.

I stared with large eyes watching until the sea of black was no longer moving and the last little creature outside and into the dark night.

"We must get some persimmons or hedge apples to attract and kill them!" came the voice of my father.

With that, off to the single bedroom, our family of four went. The crowded bedroom had two double beds. I slept with my sister who was four years older than I. There were two windows in the bedroom: one shed its light on my baby tender eight-pound body at birth. Dr. Fotch, the revered house-calling physician, had made his way to that bedroom after being summoned by my father on November 18, 1942.

"Hold this ether above your wife and dispense drops onto the cloth on her face," Dr. Fotch directed.

My father, in his nervous state, began pouring instead of dripping the pain-relieving remedy during the long and frightening dry birth. My mother and I survived the birth, but Daddy reminded me many times during my lifetime of his fear of losing my mother. I felt guilty each time.

In the adjoining room of our rented first floor, the round black coal stove chugged and puffed. At age four, I had a sizzling encounter with that coal stove. I backed into it with hands behind me. I severely burned the hand pad of my right thumb. The searing steady pain was unforgettable, but as was expected of me, I swallowed and squelched the tears as soon as possible.

This center room housed the only closet for our rental space, a low day bed, a sewing machine, the blackened round bellied coal stove, and the usual smell of coal smoke. The brown asphalt house had no modern plumbing. Water came in buckets from the cistern outside the back door where a couple of my cats waited for left over scraps of food.

"Scat, you cats. Look out!" my mother would say as she opened the door, tossed water out, or kicked my companions out of the way. The cats came and went and often had their kittens hidden away behind the old garage and near the faded grey 1935 Ford.

Since the house had no plumbing, the vegetable garden behind the house had a dusty, worn path down the middle leading to the outdoor wooden outhouse with one hole. It seemed a long way to walk or run, as the case could be, but in the winter and on inclement days, permission was granted for the use of a white chamber pot with red handle kept in the single curtained closet inside.

The exterior of this two-story house boasted a stamped brown brick-patterned asphalt siding, a porch across the front, and a single entrance front door. Inside that door, stairs rose to the second floor apartment used for other renters.

Fearsome threats designated the dark staircase with rail and wooden steps as off-limits for my sister and me. Instead, we would enter the front door hallway, quickly turn right, and go into the sitting room where the three-cushioned overstuffed sofa and a single chair sat proudly because mother had smartly outfitted and tailored the used furniture herself with a large-printed pink and blue flowered fabric.

Beside the screened back door sat the slop bucket, at least five gallons in size, containing ugly gray water and kitchen garbage that would later be fed to the hogs. The bucket had a wide enough top that I somehow fell into it when I was small. To say the least, the incident remains a nasty, humiliating but laughable memory all at the same time.

That event was in sharp contrast to the following: *Why was Uncle Arthur in our front doorway? It is so late, and he rarely comes here at all*! My four-year-old mind remembers that night, even after sixty-seven years. He stood tall, his shape filling the doorframe as the dark night surrounded him. Only the light from the single ceiling bulb showed his grim face, but he did not enter. He looked handsome; his outdoor working face had a leathery tan. He was one of my mother's brothers in a family of eleven children, all outdoor laborers or farmers.

*Why has my mother fallen straight back, nearly hitting her head on the steps that led upstairs?* I was suddenly taken aside by someone.

Something catastrophic had happened. Later, I learned that Grandfather Clouse, who once stayed with us a short time to recover from a foot injury, had left Strafford in an older model car converted to a pickup with a homemade truck bed on the back. The vehicle had been driven by Tommy, age nineteen, my mother's youngest brother. Tommy was newly married to his young and beautiful wife, Erma Lea. Grandpa Clouse, Tommy, and Erma Lea had to cross the railroad tracks en route to the Clouse home place, where all the family was born and raised. That home place was about three miles south of Strafford, Missouri. A train had struck the vehicle the three were riding in and all were instantly killed, the carnage strewn for a mile or more. The *Springfield News and Leader* reported that a fifteen-car passenger train, traveling sixty miles per hour, struck them broadside March 24, 1946, killing all three passengers.

This tragedy left only two brief visual scenes documented in my mind—the one at the door when Mother fainted and the second, a picture of three caskets at the front of Strafford Baptist church seen through my own glazed and teary eyes. Everything in those scenes appeared in sepia tones to me, absent of color and life, much like our rented home's exterior. Our family lived unknowingly in the shadowy effects of this tragedy, never spoken of.

However, in contrast to that tragic event, Mrs. Brooks—the owner of the rented brown asphalt house where we lived—had flowers. She lived next door. She was small, walked slowly, and wore dresses with brooches. We gave her the respect of her generation and age. Before our infrequent trips there, Mother always warned us, "Don't touch anything. Stay only a little while and don't pick her roses on the way back!" I liked Mrs. Brooks. And I did playfully pick petals and put them on my fingernails when we walked slowly back home.

Our brown asphalt house sat along a dirt road that led to the single school in Strafford, Missouri, a town of three hundred and later up to five hundred residents. We could easily walk the distance to school. Before I started school, I could watch the girls' drum and bugle corps as they practiced each day, marching down our nameless street. I would later lead that marching group, but not before I had served my time as a member, first playing the bell lyra, then the snare and timpani drums. Then I twirled and finally became a drum major. I liked it all, but most of all, I loved swinging the timpani drum sticks in circles as we marched, even though the heavy drum bounced harshly on my small frame and marching legs.

Living even closer to the school building and up our road were the Bumgarners.

"Oh, Alliene!" Tressa Bumgarner would exclaim in a high squealing voice as she viewed the newest gown for Eastern Star created for her by my mother. I thought our neighbors were very rich because they had a bathroom inside their house and vehicles, but especially because of the beautiful fabrics Tressa brought for mother to sew.

"Kermit makes good money," my dad would say.

Kermit drove a fuel delivery truck. Sadly, and years later, the truck rolled back and crushed him while he was underneath, repairing it. If I were asked to stay overnight there, I always hoped to take a bath in that pink tub. We used a round galvanized tub once a week at our house. Often to my disappointment, the Bumgarners plumbing did not work, so we had to use their backup outhouse anyway. Their house was white and just across the road from the brick two-story school building in which all twelve grades of Strafford School were taught. The school burned in the '60s, shortly after I graduated as valedictorian in my class of thirty-two students.

The whole town seemed to revolve around "Dear Ole Strafford High." My dad had graduated from there and was later employed as custodian for ten years. My sister graduated ahead of me in that same building in 1956. Millions of memories must still swirl in the minds of former graduates like me of that two-story old school. The tales would include Mr. Ghan, the superintendent who had faulty eyesight. Could or could he not really see who and what was going on? Mr. Ghan, in his suit and tie, stood statuesquely in the road authoritatively signaling the time for the buses to leave each day. He called me Jeannie, from my middle name, as I passed by him to walk home each day. To me, he was a huge protective and respected authority figure.

The brown asphalt house is no longer there, torn down by later school expansion, one building gobbling up the other.

*Our white house in Strafford, Missouri, on Highway 66*

# Chapter 2

## WHITE HOUSE

"Watch! It'll soon come up over the railroad tracks!" someone called out.

"The house is coming down the road now," Mrs. Alexander, my second grade teacher, said. Purchased for 1500 dollars by my parents, the white house was being moved a half mile from across the railroad tracks in Strafford and down highway 66 and onto three lots. I don't remember knowing anything about this decision to move our family or house before it happened. The whole school went to see the moving phenomenon. I was in the crowd of students somewhere, watching, but felt rather unattached since the whole change felt foreign to me. Now we would be walking further to school through rain, snow, sleet, and the hot, humid-filled fall months in Missouri.

The "new" house did not have asphalt siding. It was white painted wood and seemed to always need paint on the South side closest to the famed Highway 66 and the railroad tracks across the road. We counted railroad cars and waved at people who often waved back from the passenger trains. I wondered where the people were going since we rarely traveled from home. The three lots meant a larger garden but still, no indoor plumbing—not for another eight years. By then, I was a sophomore in high school. The upgraded outhouse did have two seats and a small window. It was pushed over backward each Halloween by prankster boyfriends. My dad would put a chain around the rickety previously owned structure, attach it to our car, and slowly bring it upright again. To me, it seemed a pretty funny mystery as to who had accomplished the task each year. I never spoke of the Halloween prank at school, hoping to deny the guilty culprits added satisfaction.

"It's your turn to wash dishes," my sister and I argued while our parents worked outside.

"No, I'll sweep the floor!"

"I like to wash. You dry," Judy said.

"You still have to get the clothes off the line!" Mother called.

Sometimes, supper time came, and Daddy was not home. The hunger pains raged while we waited for him. We never ate ahead or without him. I could swing in the porch swing, ride my green bike, read books, or practice embroidering, which I hated, but was warned by my mother to, "Stay close!"

Pets were a good diversion while we waited. We had Fluffo (a gray cat), Henny and Penny (banty roosters), and dogs named Wimpy, Coalie, and Cindy. One by one, they joined the memorial pet cemetery complete with white hand-painted boards, bearing each one's name. I taught Cindy, a cute little terrier of some sort, to "talk." She could say, "Howl-o!" (translated "hello"). We saw some dogs on television that had been trained to talk. I wanted to get her on TV, so I worked with her ambitiously and gave her tiny cookie treats as she performed. I was sure she could do that one word.

We raised chickens and had eggs to sell and eat. These chickens were not pets. They scared me when they squawked on nests of eggs. Nonetheless, we fed and watered them and gathered eggs. The egg money turned into piano-lesson money. Dora Jean Austin, who lived a long bike ride away off Highway 66, gave us lessons. Some eggs eventually settled into the front basket of the used green bike we got for Christmas to make the weekly long ride to the Austin house.

In the white house, the best memory for me with a chicken theme was a special time with my father as we shingled the roof on the chicken house together. Eager to be the best helper, I worked beside him as I did on another occasion when we put a floor in the attic of the house. The tongue and groove boards of white pine were badly bowed. My job was to use the hammer and chisel ahead of Daddy to straighten or pry the curving boards so he could nail them. I felt that he was happy with my help. I felt appreciated and grown up on both the building and repair jobs. The floored attic of the white house would hold a bit of everything including my savings, nickels in a jar, being put aside for college money.

No one had ever gone to college on either side of my parents' families that we knew of. My sister was the first. She fell in love with David and married after her first year, later to finish and complete twenty years in the public classroom as an elementary school teacher.

My desire to go to college came from my commitment to someday become a missionary. I read biographies of early missionaries such as Adoniram Judson, the first English missionary to Burma (now Myanmar) who translated the Bible into Burmese, a translation still used today. I had read and studied requirements from the Foreign Mission Board, and they said that a woman should have a degree in English and history to equip her to teach her children, if she married and lived abroad. That was all the direction I needed. *I must go to college, and I will somehow.* I determined.

Hot and humid Missouri nights hummed with katydids and sparkled with lightning bugs. We put the fireflies in glass bottles to see how long their light would glow, or we mashed the glow part onto our fingers and let our fingers dance about in the dark. Some evenings, it was so hot that the best place to be was outside. The sky and the moon seemed like my close friends just as my God was a friend to me. The man in the moon looked like a side view of Mary with Jesus in its darker shadowed part. I could not see the man but would often let my heart be touched by the awesome bigness of the sky, universe, and thoughts of God.

One day in the white house, I must have asked my mother a question about God, Jesus, salvation, heaven, or hell. The exact question is not remembered, but the picturesque situation remains. Mother invited me to our knees in the dining room where the heating stove sat. It was totally quiet. I had never heard my mother pray aloud, but I knew she was praying silently. I wondered why we were there and looked around, memorizing the creases in the red hassock we knelt beside. We were there for a while before getting up. They say that we all are the result of someone's prayers for us. Sometime later, a few days before my ninth birthday in November 1951, Strafford Baptist Church had a revival, a series of nightly meetings that would often last two weeks. My salvation experience came after a terrible wind and lightning storm during which I promised Jesus that I would be saved by inviting Him to be my own Savior, if only I lived through the storm. I knew I wanted to go to heaven.

The storm raged as we went to bed. *Please let me live so I can go to the front of the church and be saved*, I prayed. Just for good measure, I also prayed the Lord's Prayer I had memorized earlier. The wind was blowing so hard that I not only heard the sound of it but also could see the linoleum puff and rise from the floor and go down again as I finally and fearfully closed my eyes to sleep.

The next evening at the end of the revival service, I told my mother that I was going to go up to the front of the church during the invitation. I was determining my own eternal fate and felt quite respected in this spiritual matter because Mother did not stop me. From the moment my feet touched the aisle, I felt as if I were floating. I don't remember walking. I don't recall the name of the woman who talked with me or the scriptures from the Bible she read. I do remember that my almost–nine-year-old heart was broken with a new awareness of sin and the need for a loving Father to rescue me. I cried my heart out in repentance as if I were the worst of all sinners and, afterward, floated back down the aisle to the back door where the pastor picked me up into his arms.

"I am as light as a feather!" I remember telling him because that is how I felt in my heart and body. I would later marry in the same white church with big half oval windows and large stuccoed pillars on the long front porch. Those pillars reminded me of guards, looking over where I had played and worshipped as a child.

*Strafford Baptist Church, Strafford, Missouri*

# Chapter 3

## CHURCH

Strafford Baptist Church was the one my sister and I cleaned for many years. We made fifteen dollars a month. I got seven dollars and fifty cents of that money each month, and we cleaned the building every Saturday.

"Don't you tell on me!" I cried to Judy.

Judy was crumpled on the front pew. *Had I really shoved her that hard?* I was scared. Her head hit the corner of a wooden moveable speaking stand. I had pushed her. She hid her face with her hands and the real fear of God came over me. I began to bargain all sorts of things.

"Just don't tell. Please, please, please!" I said with terrified urgency.

We had the whole building to ourselves, so it was a good place for airing our grievances, if we had some or if we just wanted to be mean. I was definitely sorry I had pushed her and fearful at the same time, while surprising myself with my own deliberate actions. She didn't tell on me, but I still look for a tiny scar on her face sometimes when we are together, and I remember.

The basement of Strafford Baptist Church was an ugly place because it was dark, damp, always chilly, and smelled of mildew. The excavation for the basement was done by hand underneath the building, and the dirt was moved out one wheel barrow at a time up an incline. The dirt was reddish clay. Once, the basement flooded, and the men put a sump pump in the corner. The stairway space to the basement was taken out of the Southwest side of the small auditorium. Underneath the stairway in the basement was storage for paper leftovers, props, curtains, literature, and craft items from Vacation Bible School. That ill-lit jumble of junk beneath the stairway was an insurmountable organizational straightening task to this ten-year-old! What could be done? I often thought. I could sweep with the big oiled mop or broom, dust, and arrange chairs for Sunday classrooms handily and sometimes proudly make a slight dent in the conglomerate under the stairs. I liked to shine and dust the piano but generally did not like the time that the cleaning took every weekend, dreading the hours we spent there.

Remarkably, that basement became a type of memorial in my life. As a memorial to remember what God had done, the Israelites carried stones from the Red Sea to remind them of God's deliverance from Egypt. As clear as a ringing bell, I remember one "stone-carrying" occasion that happened in that basement.

I had read of missionaries who told about the sacrifices they made, often losing children and wives to prevalent diseases. I read about the Elliots who were murdered by the Auca Indians in South America and whose family went back to forgive and see salvation come to this group of cannibalistic natives. *Through Gates of Splendor* by Elizabeth Elliot chronicles this story. Girls Auxiliary, a new mission program for young girls, had put me in touch with a missionary in Japan, Doris Spencer. She wrote me back when I wrote her and told me about the needs around the world and her life. I was falling in love with Japan. In my youth, I feared that being a missionary would mean that I would be single and not have children. That made me sad. I did not want that. Yet every time I read or heard anything about telling people in foreign lands about Jesus, my heart was so stirred within me. It was a calling felt strongly in my heart.

I questioned what I felt so strongly. I cried more. One day, in that dark basement, I was so tormented by the idea of surrender to this call on my life that I knelt at a fold-up bench on the cold concrete floor and cried my heart out as I struggled with what I was feeling and the fears that accompanied them. I rose, still with tears and a wet face, and began to straighten a wooden desk whose rolled-top was missing. As I was dusting the large area, a blue plastic bookmark flipped over, and I picked it up to read what was printed on it. I read, "'For we know that all things work together for the good to those who love the Lord, to those called according to His purpose' Romans 8:28 (KJV)." Those words hit me as if straight from heaven, and I experienced sudden relief and joy! My prayers and struggle were heard and understood. I relaxed in knowing that all would work together for good. I smiled, laughed, and cried happy tears this time. Sometime after that, I wrote the Foreign Mission Board and asked about requirements for becoming a missionary. I told no one, especially my parents, whom I feared would dissuade me from what I was now happily committed to do. As letters arrived back and if I expected one, I would wait and watch at the mailbox on the road. The mission board said I should write a biography to be kept on file at that point. I could continue to write other missionaries. I could go to college and major in English and history in case I were to marry and have to teach my children. I was eleven years old.

The little white church became a leadership training ground as I studied the Bible, did advanced steps in Girls Auxiliary, taught children, sang with my sister and in the choir, and served as president and other offices in classes or youth groups. My commitment to missions was a strong incentive for school and work. In high school, I took English and Latin, read poetry in forensic competitions and had roles in dramatic plays. I definitely did not like social studies. However, social studies was better than learning to tell time in the third grade. Those clock arms and placement diagrams that we drew were a frustrating mystery to me. I do not recall my parents ever asking about or helping with my homework. They were busy providing food, clothes, and housing. Mother, as a seamstress, made our clothes until I began to work and had some money to help buy my own.

I began saving nickels for college at a young age out of the church cleaning money even though college did not seem financially possibly. I carefully spent money from tips I made at the drive-in, my first job. I was scared at that job though. Making change was the second mystery like telling time had been. Once I dropped a whole tray of fresh hamburgers onto the floor in front of hungry customers I was serving. I was so embarrassed and sorry, but the largest tip I ever received followed that order—a five-dollar bill! During my sophomore summer of high school, I proudly bought a pair of wool type dark aqua pants that zipped on the side with money I earned. They had tapered legs.

My second job that helped me through college was at Heer's Department Store in Springfield, Missouri. My tired feet and aching legs after eight hours of work were the worst part of that job. We wore navy or black, in the summer beige, and always some type of high heels. The best part of work was payday, a regular check, and the layaway plan that enlarged my wardrobe with Jantzen honey bun sweaters and skirts to match. In my early days at Heer's, I was often given a job of handing out promotional materials or coupons at the front door. When I worked until closing at night, the walk to the dark parking lot and drive home on icy roads faced my immaturity and youth squarely. Nevertheless, the working effort helped the college fund and new bank account.

Strafford Baptist Church, work, and school were all directed toward my goal and of monumental importance in my life. At that church, I met Jesus. I answered a call to foreign missions there. I was trained as a leader there. I was sent as a summer missionary to the Northwestern United States in 1962 along with three others from there. I married Don Spurgeon there in 1964. I carried a memorial stone from there.

# Chapter 4

## MISSION IN A DRAWER

My sister Judy, almost five years older than I, could sing. When I was four years old and she, almost nine, we were asked to sing together at our small church. I believe the song was "Whispering Hope." The words I am hearing now:

> "Soft as the voice of an angel, breathing a lesson unheard,
>
> Hope with a gentle persuasion; whispers her comforting word:
>
> Wait till the darkness is over, wait till the tempest is done,
>
> Hope for the sunshine tomorrow after the shower is gone.
>
> Whispering hope, oh how welcome thy voice,
>
> Making my heart in its sorrow rejoice."

Jane Handley was a good singer in the church choir at Strafford and often sang solos. In other words, everyone respected her as the best musician. On one particular Sunday, she sought me out with a question.

"How did you learn to sing alto? Did you know you were singing the harmony?" she asked.

I answered no to both questions. I wasn't sure how to respond or what she was asking me. I was too young to know, but my ears must have heard the alto harmony naturally. I just knew that I stood there in my taffeta dress with Judy and sang. It was a type of beginning, a short chapter really, but I can still find that hymn in an old green Broadman hymnal copyrighted 1940. About the third drawer down in a bedroom dresser, that songbook, as we called them, joins a host of others. Some of the pages are yellowed with age and have wrinkled leather like paperbacks where the creases no longer show the printing. One paperbacked song book has the name of my uncle Thomas, called Tommy, who died in the tragic truck and train accident. The signature is handwritten by him. The copyright is in numeral letters MCMXXIX, 1929. The book, edited and published by R. E. Winset, says it is "a book of songs that charm, edify, win the heart, touch the soul and last." And so many dear hymns have lasted as did the cross drawn with orange crayon filling the lines on the back of the book. The crayon reminds me that there was no childcare provided at church so children busied themselves in sometimes very long services sitting beside their parents.

At about age ten, when asked what I wanted for any upcoming occasion, I always said, "I want a horse and a piano!" The horse did not happen, but eventually, a used upright piano found its way into our small Strafford living room, and piano lessons began with the egg money. Dora Jean began with scales; Hanon, finger exercises; and John Schwann, books with learning levels identified by colored books. Our lesson always ended with a hymn from the church hymn book. Dora Jean would sometimes play it for me so I could hear it first. Hearing it played first was a great help.

Piano recitals followed as did learning to play the clarinet, oboe, singing in school choir ensembles, and playing in band and orchestra. Performances made me extremely anxious, and my sweaty hands outdid themselves with nervously dripping moisture from my palms. My father would say to me, "No one will want to hold those hands."

Solos for competition filled my time with practices. Rhythm and tone were not a problem. Looking at my parental examples, my mother did not sing much but did yodel and whistle while she worked. Daddy sang in the church choir and later played his harmonica till he was ninety-six years old. I dearly remember my grandmother placing her short fingers on the old pump organ keys and stretching her tiny short legs out to touch her feet to the pedals. She played by ear and occasionally by shaped notes.

Vocal music seemed to win out in the end. I led the music for youth group and church services in high school and college. That suited me more than single performances. But the duets I began with my sister lasted for many years as did the duets with Don after we married.

Early on, our music library consisted of hymnals, duet books in various voices, the "Youth Sings" chorus books, and a few classic pieces of sheet music including "Rustic Dance," "Norwegian Concerto," "O Holy Night," "Cantique de Noel," and others.

It was a definite break in tradition when we first heard Ethel Waters, George Beverly Shea, Tennessee Ernie Ford, and the choirs at church practice from some sheet music and not solely from the hymnal. Until the 1960s, the songs were written by greats such as John Wesley and Fanny Crosby. "This Old House," "It is No Secret," "Until Then," by Stuart Hamlin, "Do You Really Care?" and soon after "Because He Lives" were followed by hundreds of Bill and Gloria Gaither songs. It was hard to keep up. Christian television had not surfaced or iPods, or even cassette tapes at that point. So when someone heard a new song, every one sang it in their own version, many times over. We did the same with "He Touched Me" and "There Is a River." One of the early ones Don and I sang together was "Heaven Came Down and Glory Filled My Soul" by John Peterson who wrote and arranged many church cantata musicals. At Christmas, Don and I sang "Ring the Bells, Ring the Bells" with words, "Let the whole world know" and later, "Wise Men Still Adore Him."

I would go to the Christian bookstore in search of the few background cassettes available. We began to collect a few. We preferred a piano accompanist except for weddings or funerals since it was easier to practice together at home with a cassette. Our children were accustomed to hearing the same song over and over and over again as we practiced. I was the perfectionist and hated missed notes or uncertainty in harmony. We became rather innovative and often switched parts within a song as in "It Is Finished" and "A Perfect Heart." Those precious words became very dear. "I Believe in a Hill Called Mt. Calvary" and "The Old Rugged Cross Made the Difference" was a medley that Don sang as a solo many times.

In one drawer down in that dresser there lies a thick black three-ringed binder with lined notebook pages. Glued onto the sheets or handwritten with chords by phrases are words to and sometimes music cut from other books to make up the scripture-based songs we came to love and sing. "Now Unto the King Eternal" from 2 Timothy was one of the first taken word for word from scripture. It seems those words and melody are printed in my mind indelibly.

In my thirties, I taught myself to play the autoharp while trying to get well after a long-standing battle with incapacitating physical symptoms in my chest. With the autoharp, certain chords were possible when keys were pushed and strummed at the same time. The black case that held the autoharp matched the black-ringed binder, which became my lesson book of songs that I learned for the autoharp. Don and I sang many of those songs together at church, but my fear of disrupting the whole song with missed or totally "off" chords basically ended that performance chapter. Between 1975 and 1985, we became a part of a choir that began giving performances first at Calvary Community Church and then the Great Falls Civic Center now known as the Mansfield Center of Performing Arts.

"Turn to page 27!" Renae shouted.

"Now to 49!" she continued.

With basses, tenors, altos, sopranos separated for a short time in their own space, the problem areas were pounded out on the piano week after week, quickly. Renae led us like no other person we have known. Prayer was an important part of each performance so that by the time the curtain rose on marvelous sets, lights, and the hard work of so many, the mission to the community was usually communicated by God's grace with excellence. That chapter is not in the drawers of the dresser because by this time, we were into the era of cassette tapes. Everyone used the tapes to learn parts and the final performance was recorded onto cassettes. These productions took a lot of time! Our Christmas tree did not go up until the last performance at the Civic Center ended since our extra time was given to memorizing and practicing from September to December. With a short break, Easter productions and practices resumed. The time it took to prepare was enormous, but fulfilling and worth it.

"All my debts cancelled," sang Don as he stood, looking taller than ever in his costume that draped to the floor while he lifted his hands to heaven and the choir resounded behind him. Though that season and chapter have closed, the triumphant melodies linger.

More Christmases and more Easters followed and then came the Fourth of July Patriotic Celebrations in Gibson Park. Joel, a friend, once told Don after a vocal solo, "You didn't even embarrass me!"

Occasionally, I sit at the piano and play the old hymns or songs I once knew from memory or the beloved songs from the Bible. My confidence in my own ability to hear and pick and be blessed while at the piano is a relaxing coming together of all those years that started when I rode my bike to piano lessons or went to the summer program at school to learn an instrument.

There is one more chapter in that music drawer. It has "fun" written all over it. For some reason that escapes me, I called several vocal music teachers and purchased a set of voice lessons for Don and me and gave it to us as an anniversary gift. We laughed as we drove to our lesson and practiced our scales and limbered our vocal cords before we got there. The exercises and warm ups made us sound silly. After singing alto all those previous years, the teacher decided I was really a soprano, which never felt comfortable to me. But we did our part in the recital and sang a couple of songs but did not join the symphony when asked! I'm glad we took those lessons.

Our oneness as a couple was often challenged before we sang. There were nerves, crumpled papers with lyrics written on them, practices, and songs en route in the car. There were the last-minute changes and double checks on the memorized words as well. And, yes, there were arguments that ended when and after the lingering notes surrendered to the reason for singing in the first place. We memorized at least half of the songs we sang. We often held hands to keep us together in time with each other as we sang, and a part of the ministry in song seemed to be the oneness demonstrated as a couple who loved each other. Those opportunities blessed us and our marriage. On any occasion, our song could be, "I will sing of the mercies of the Lord, forever; I will sing, I will sing" Psalm 89:1, (KJV).

# Chapter 5

## SCHOOLS

Classes at Strafford High School included all twelve grades with no kindergarten. I started school when I was five and attended all twelve grades there in one building. Beginning with the first grade swat from Mrs. McGee because I was late coming in the door from recess and ending with the valedictory speech of the graduating class on May of 1960, my somewhat-protected life seemed complete to me. I didn't like Mr. Alexander, the biology teacher, and was a bit afraid of Miss Ross, the English teacher, but all the others seemed to do their job and pass us along. Miss Page, the single music teacher, took me aside in the eighth grade to ask me to play the bell lyre in the all-girl drum and bugle corps. She had already moved me past the clarinet in band and orchestra to a school-owned elderly oboe. I would not have considered saying no to Miss Page even though each change was new and uncomfortable. I was unsure of my abilities in both and felt embarrassed at my mistakes. She often picked me to direct the band or orchestra during the last several minutes of practice time. I loved that! It seemed natural, and I was sorry to hear the bell ring. During my senior year, I was asked by the Southwest Missouri State College Band to play the oboe with their band. I had real doubts about playing there and felt I contributed very little, but Miss Page, with the round face and body, seemed to think I was okay. That certainly encouraged me.

Band, orchestra, drum and bugle corps, yearbook, Student Council, plays, choirs, ensembles, solos, and forensic competitions along with bookkeeping and math blurred my life with activity. Latin, a seemingly nonprofitable subject and less than exciting class, ended up satisfying some foreign language credit in college and helped me pronounce Hawaii, Honoapilani, Haleakala, and my beloved Napili Bay in much later years.

The boys I dated during high school had to attend Saturday night youth group at Strafford Baptist Church. My friend Patsy played the piano, and I usually led in some fashion. I also invited guest speakers. Many boyfriends did not pass the test of understanding my mission's call, and as a result, sad good-byes seemed inevitable and were.

My parents seemed unattached to my efforts and hard work in all those school and church activities. They were busy. They rarely attended the programs or performances. Mother would say, "Pretty is pretty does," all the time to me as some kind of instruction, which I did not understand. We had arguments about trust issues. My trust in mother's love had been shaken already by her harsh childhood discipline. There was the paddle, the belt, the yardstick, the bruises, and embarrassment that caused me to talk about her when I went to my friend Patsy's house and compare my mother with hers. I thought my mother was mean. I later walked through that troubling baggage with forgiveness and understanding left only with one regret, that as I matured, I could have related more openly, loved, and touched my mother as she so needed. She was herself a product of a harsh family past seldom spoken of.

Thirty-five or forty miles away from Strafford seemed like a long distance to me. That was where Southwest Baptist College (now University) was located. It was a Christian junior college at Bolivar Missouri and offered a five-hundred-dollar scholarship, which I picked up. The first two weeks, I was homesick for the first time in my life. It was an aching type feeling, foreign and strange, lonely and empty. However, very soon, I stood in a line and met a sophomore student going to Mission's Club specifically for mission volunteers. *That is me. I am a volunteer! Was this the man?* I wondered as a seventeen-year-old. No, he wasn't. At college, I felt hopeful and in charge but also careful and cautious. College independence was good for me. When I visited home after that, I was respected, for the most part. Even the boys I dated were accepted by my parents.

Blue Home where I lived was an old house with a long wide wrap-around front porch. The house was white though and later painted blue. I had three roommates at the start of my freshman year. There was one small closet for all of us, a single mattress on springs for each, and only one community bathroom for the thirteen girls who lived on second floor. The beautiful winding staircase started in the front room where a piano sat. Our housemother, Mrs. Riley, lived with her daughter in another front room. I greatly admired her daughter, Sandra, and wished to be like her. I did follow her in some ways as evening Vespers Chairman and later "Miss Southwest." Each evening, students were invited to a short devotional quiet time following the evening meal. I planned and organized these for several months. The atmosphere at SWBC from fall to graduation in May was the best possible for a first year of college. Chapel with required attendance happened every day, and other special emphasis weeks were devoted to finding God's will for our lives. One of those times occurred in my life during a Spiritual Life Focus Week, which took me to the upstairs attic at Blue Home where I prayed quietly. I prayed a long time, and I experienced a new commitment to follow this Savior wherever He led. Just being able to attend college was a miracle, and my parents knew it. That small nickel fund, the scholarship, my part-time work, and the money God provided from my parents allowed those two years to happen.

My dad once said to me, "I don't know where the money came from."

After junior college, I signed up with the Home Mission Board to be a summer missionary. This meant serving for ten weeks, assigned to anywhere in the United States. The pay was $200 total for ten weeks, which was a sacrifice for me as I knew I could work for more at my summer job with Heer's Department Store. But this was also a chance to experience what I felt called to do in my life. During those years, I had gone on three revival teams to small Missouri churches from SWBC during my time there. I would usually direct the music on these teams.

The team would also share their Christian testimonies in the services or teach wherever needed. The sleeping arrangements on these teams were always a surprise. Once, we stayed with a very poor family. I slept with one of their daughters in the same bed and felt the wind whistle through the boards in the wall onto my face. There was a pig that ran through the house, and there was scarcely enough basic food for that weekend. It was a cultural shock that made me dream of my dorm room, but wait—some "dear" friends had lovingly toilet-papered the whole room before I got back to campus, crisscrossing carefully throughout. I cried when I saw the mess. So silly. This was my "mansion" by comparison to what I had experienced on the weekend. Is this what missions in a foreign country would feel like?

*White and Black Oxfords*

*Don Spurgeon, Carol Davolt, 1960 Southwest Baptist College*

# Chapter 6

## WHITE AND BLACK OXFORDS

They called it "twirp" week at Southwest Baptist College, now University. The girls could ask the fellas out. That was a first for me, and I did not have anyone in mind to ask until I saw this handsome guy sitting on the floor next to a block wall in Maupin dining hall at the twirp week kick-off party. He had a flat top hairstyle, and I noticed his sunglasses and beige jacket. Maybe I had seen him before, but I definitely noticed him that night. Suddenly, he was missing, and I ran to the door and outside with the maybe intentions of "twirping" him. He was already walking toward the men's dorm. It was dark out, but in the campus light, I saw the white of the saddle oxford shoes he wore. I watched. My heart raced a bit at my boldness in running after him. I didn't try to catch up with him. I missed my chance and felt disappointed. Or was I relieved?

Word got around on the small campus. I found out his name and managed to talk a bit in the foyer of the dining hall with him. He was a basketball player, so he ate either before or after everyone else because of his basketball practice schedule, but on occasion, I could see him at lunch. Enter, Don Alt Spurgeon.

Our first date was on a Sunday night. We went to church at First Baptist. That night, he wore a gray green plaid wool sport jacket, and we sat close to the back of the church on the left side. He was so tall that his caring mother had his sport coats measured and tailored at Aufderheide's in Owensville, Missouri. I was impressed. He was born in St. Louis and raised in Owensville sixty-five miles south and west. It seemed I was impressed by everything about him, even his cool-somewhat-aloof manner. During that time, I dated anyone who asked me first, so—as Don recalls—I had a breakfast walk-back-to-dorm date, a church date, a Coke date in the afternoon, and another date in the evening, all with different boys. He was not sure he wanted to compete. He dated others also, and one of his roommates had told me that I had better get off the fence or lose him. So my roommate Becky and I devised a plan. I wrote a note, which she delivered to Don at basketball practice, saying I would like to see him. How bold of me!

We had some great walks from early breakfast to Blue Home. I am still amazed I got up so early to make it to breakfast, but I did it because I loved being with him. We were falling in love. I had a long coat with a huge collar. He would sometimes pull the collar around my face and kiss me good-bye. We had Old Testament History together. We sat together. Some of Old Testament History did not "sink in." One time, he asked me for a date after class, and I became so flustered that I walked down a ramp into another class in session, blushing as I made my hurried back-up exit.

Very early in our dating, I had explained my plans to be a missionary to Don, and that I was a mission's volunteer. We prayed together about this on every date after that. It was always in my mind somewhere. But as we looked dazedly into each other's eyes, we fell more in love. We would pray that if God did not want us together, we would know it and part quickly. It seemed now a tough assignment, even for God, given our "moving right along" romance. I visited his home. He visited my home, and by March of 1961, we had decided to date only each other, which we did for the next three years and three months to our wedding day, Friday, June 13, 1964. I graduated from college one week. We married the next week while he was a second year dental student at Washington University School of Dentistry in St. Louis. It seemed we had waited forever.

While apart during those dating years, we wrote letters to each other every day and called only about every two to three weeks because it was expensive for long-distance calls. Somehow, we did see each other about every other month although we were both consumed with the pressures of classes, especially Don. It was a difficult time for our long-distance romance because we really wanted to be together. I needed to be able to support us while he finished dental school, so I needed my teaching degree.

To me, Don was perfect. My parents fell in love with him too, so before I knew it, he asked my Dad and Mother about giving me a ring. They said yes. In March of 1963, I went to St. Louis for a weekend visit. He took me into his bedroom, put his letter jacket from Drury College over my head, got out the ring, and knelt down on one knee as he opened the ring box. Then the jacket came off my head, and he asked me to marry him. I literally shook for days as I looked at that beautiful ring, knowing what it meant—a lifelong commitment. Our good-byes were very tearful.

After we married, we had a short honeymoon to Kimberly City near Branson where Don got the worst sunburn of his life while removing the white shoe polish marriage congratulatory remarks off the 64 Chevrolet Biscayne. Don had two more years of school, so I moved to St. Louis to become Mrs. Don Spurgeon. I also became Mrs. Spurgeon, teacher of sophomore and junior English in a school of four thousand at Ritenour Senior High School. We were still praying together.

*Our first home, Marvin Gardens, St. Louis, Missouri*

# Chapter 7

## APARTMENT LIFE DECISIONS

Marvin Gardens in St. Louis was an apartment complex. I liked the name. Was it because Gardens sounded romantic enough to be our first home? Maybe. The building was one-story with four apartments in each building. All the floors had asbestos square tile, and we had a front and back door with screens and a clothesline in the back we shared with neighbors. Three rooms in all, a bathroom, and the tiny kitchen were enough for me to nurture and discover any homemaking skills I might have. Marvin Gardens was a real first in many ways.

In the cooking department, I remember well the eggs I boiled for our breakfast because I could start them while getting ready for school. Don remembers them even better. Once, I labored with cookbook author, Betty Crocker over a ham when we were having company. I have never again fixed that mustard sauce that went on the top. Sorry, Betty! My early cooking skills were not the best, but I continued with the help of a pressure cooker, a wedding gift that did quite well with the pinto beans we had regularly. We survived, and my tall, handsome husband did not complain, or does he now.

On another occasion, the meatball recipe that came right from my high school home economics class was served to the Majorettes I sponsored at Ritenour High School. This was a group I could be friendlier with since I had determined not to smile for six months while teaching in my regular English classes because I was afraid that as a first-time teacher, I would not be taken seriously. I was serious, I guess. I had no discipline problems except Jon who challenged me so much that I wanted to hit him when he refused to raise his head from the desk where he sat, totally able but unwilling to be a student.

That first apartment was furnished with a few donations from Don's family. There was the used bed and frame and a gray and chrome Formica table. Two oak dining chairs came from the Niebreugge farm that we repaired and refinished. In the kitchen, I made some curtains from a green-striped sheet and attached white detachable hanger grips to slide onto a white metal rod. Our concrete block and board bookcase was one of the first building projects we ever accomplished. The used fifteen-dollar fold out foam-cushioned couch was definitely the best buy. On a visit to Marvin Gardens, Mother hand-stitched a handkerchief over a tear on the underside of the brown cushion. Don's twin bed from college days was in the living room corner. We had a small black-and-white TV also, from which I began to see more sports than I had ever seen in my life.

For some reason, I thought the tile floors in the apartment needed to be waxed often. So I did. The washers—no dryers—were about a half block away and wet clothes in baskets challenged my never-a-thought-about fitness stamina and strength. I knew how to iron from an early start at home. Don had many shirts to iron because dental students wore dress shirts and ties. My new wife thinking included the idea that I was to iron them all, and I resented Don's mother somewhat when she asked if she could iron them instead of me. My own mother wisely said, "Let her iron his shirts!" So I yielded my ironing status while he finished school.

One of the first decisions we made as a couple had to do with church attendance and tithing, even on the small living salary we had. God led us to Christ Memorial Baptist Church just off the freeway near Florissant Road. It was high on a hill and a wonderful place to be. We loved our Pastor, Bill Little, who also taught the young married adults Sunday School Class. It was there that we heard and experienced conversational prayer as a group. We simplified the whole preconceived praying thing and just talked to Jesus, each one, back and forth by subjects—a practice we taught and used for many years then and later also. We sang our first duets in that church and grew in Christ in many ways. The sermons always stirred us toward commitment and inspired us.

Just two years prior when I was a summer missionary in the Northwest, the summer of 1962 between my sophomore and junior years in college, I became very aware of God's faithfulness. I wrote in my diary on the long return train ride: "Lord, if you ever want me to serve you again in this beautiful area of the country, I am willing." It was not the foreign mission field, but my response to missions anywhere was as sincere as that first surrender as the ten or eleven-year-old girl in the basement of Strafford Baptist Church. I applied to the Home Mission Board to help in vacation Bible schools and to take censuses for the Southern Baptist Convention. That experience was eye-opening, especially for a girl who had never traveled past Arkansas or Iowa, seen the Rocky Mountains, the city of Seattle hosting the World's Fair, or the Columbia River Gorge. The fifty-four hours on the train each way, although long, was time to make that surrendered prayer.

Fifty years later, we are often asked, "How did you guys get to Montana?" We believe now, as we did then, that God directs our steps when we seek Him, and we did that together. We prayed a lot.

So here we were peering at a map, realizing the time had come to leave the first home and our little brick apartment at Marvin Gardens. In June 1966, Don became a credentialed licensed doctor of dentistry and graduate of Washington University Dental School, with a Doctor of Dental Surgery now in place after his name. For him, it was four years of really hard, pressured medical studies, with laboratories and many, many exams and levels of qualifications to pass. He graduated over the mid percentile in his class.

"Where is Malmstrom, Montana?" we quizzed each other when the orders came from Uncle Sam and the United States Air Force.

Don had enlisted two years earlier while he was in dental school, and those years counted toward his four-year commitment. Stretching a large US map across the gray formica kitchen table, we located Montana first, then Great Falls, and in smaller print, Malmstrom AFB. We felt strangely as if we had just been sent from our families to an unknown foreign land. But the Northwest was one of our choices when we filled out applications for the US Air Force. My summer in the Northwest for ten weeks in 1962 was so life-changing and memorable that together, we felt God was directing our path. He hears every breath of prayer in a human heart or mouth. Don and I believed together that God was sending us to the right place even though it was a strange feeling to think of leaving Missouri.

I had completed my second year of teaching English at Ritenour High School, which was one of the scariest seasons of my life. Teaching was scary because I felt inadequate in my abilities to teach, and since I was such a committed perfectionist, the high demands I put on students and myself were somehow viewed by the administration as my being able to teach accelerated students my second year. I had made teaching very intense and consuming.

The move was sounding better and better. Besides that, it was definitely time to leave for another reason. We were smitten by the strong desire to have a baby and start our family!

*Beige Military Housing, Malmstrom AFB, Montana*

# Chapter 8

## MILITARY BEIGE

Black Eagle, Montana, probably was not our first choice of places to live in Great Falls. No housing was available on the base at the time we arrived in August 1966. We were placed on a waiting list. We packed what would fit into the '64 turquoise Biscayne Chevy. When Don finished at Shepherd AFB, Wichita Falls, Texas, and after brief visits with family along the way, we headed north and west. The scenery was amazing with little stops near Jackson, Wyoming, and Yellowstone. Taking the scenic drive to Great Falls, we followed little mountain streams, hoping that Great Falls would be so beautiful.

We were wide-eyed first-timers finding our way around the base and Great Falls. The owner of the 3-D Club in Black Eagle had half a trailer available for rent. It was behind a service station on gravel and near the Missouri River. *Why do I remember smelling onions? Or was it the oil refinery on fifteenth street nearby?* When Don left for the base each morning, it meant that my day was spent listening to the sound of the refinery and experiencing the nostril-deadening crude oil smell in the air. Was this Montana? It certainly was not the beautiful creek in the mountains we passed on our drive here. Loneliness visited me like an unwelcomed neighbor's dog. Things did get better though, when we took a weekend trip to Glacier National Park. Neither of us had ever seen anything like the landscapes we saw there. It was early September by then, and although it was cold in the cabin we rented, the beauty was astounding. Of course, I didn't know it yet, but I came back pregnant, which may explain why I was so sensitive in remembering the smells in Black Eagle.

Finally, our wait for housing was over, and our living standards definitely improved when we were assigned base housing. Imagine this: a garage, three bedrooms, large living-dining room, two bathrooms, large kitchen, and a basement too. Our address, 4936 A. Locust, on the perimeter of the base, allowed us to see the famous Anaconda smokestack in Black Eagle that stood a tall six hundred feet in the air sporting its plume of smoke drifting toward the North. We could see it across the Missouri River from our big living room windows. All of Great Falls loved the stack, a direction guide for any confused traveler. I immediately envisioned our Christmas tree in that big living room window with the smokestack as a backdrop.

Absent of furniture, the entry, a closet, a long hall, hardwood floors, tile in the bathrooms, and the empty basement sounded very hollow as we viewed it, trying to imagine what we would do with all that space. We did not have a stick of furniture or appliances to absorb the sound except an electric skillet brought from St. Louis and a few linens. When we received our travel paycheck, we lavishly ordered bedroom furniture and bought a sofa at Town and Ranch Furniture Store. On nearly the same day, we bought our first washer and dryer at Sears.

As we left Sears, in downtown Great Falls, and prepared to cross Third Street going west to find our car, nausea overtook me. It was a constant nausea, signaling the first signs of what seemed to us a long-awaited pregnancy. Those two bathrooms on Locust became well-known to me as I practiced, "*Thank you, Jesus, for this baby,*" and heaved into the toilet surrounded by pale green-gray tile. The color was appropriate for the way I felt for the first six months in the military beige duplex.

I had not been pregnant when I left a Christian Women's Club luncheon held at the Rainbow Hotel a few months prior. On the way back to the base, I parked beside the Missouri River at the beautiful Black Eagle falls overlook. While there, I literally cried out in desperation to the Lord for a child. I gave the child back to Him at the same time. It was a significant moment in my life and with my Lord. Jeff was conceived a short time afterward, a real answer to prayer. His middle name would be Alt to become the third generation of Alts started by Don's Grandfather Spurgeon, a "horse and buggy" doctor in Red Bird, Missouri, who named several sons after professors at his medical school at the Beaumont Medical College, St. Louis. The name Alt is now carried to the fourth generation.

I sewed maternity clothes, and the church gave me a surprise baby shower. There was much love and anticipation for this baby who came in May, the day after Mother's Day, May 15, 1967. He had the biggest eyes we had ever seen. Don said he was the most beautiful baby in the world. He was a long 7 lbs 12 oz boy. I was stunned with this overwhelming new responsibility and became a serious mother, following the *Better Homes and Garden* manual on about everything including the one, two, threes of bathing a baby from cotton balls for the eyes to Q-tips for the nose. Poor baby, to be loved so much. There were a few complications after his birth, and nursing was a challenge. In those days, almost every newborn baby was bottle-fed, with no support groups for breastfeeding. We had not encouraged family to come help us, so we did our best. The military beige house had baby sounds in it now and puppy sounds too. Greta, a black cockapoo, had joined us about three months before Jeffrey Alt's birth.

When Jeff started having some juices from a bottle, an extremely frightening ordeal happened. He liked the sweet taste of course, and the liquid was sucked easily from the Playtex nursing bottle. He drank too quickly, and too much went down too fast. I was alone in the kitchen, holding him and giving him this juice when he became choked and could not breathe. His already large eyes bulged, and his face reddened. It was an emergency. He could not breathe. The phone was on the wall beside me, but I couldn't remember any numbers. I began punching any numbers, hoping someone would answer. I needed help immediately! I dropped the phone and squeezed him as I cried out, "*God, this is my baby!*" I squeezed again and again, and after what seemed forever, a few tiny bubbles came from his little mouth. I grabbed him and started running to the front door for help. As I reached for the handle on the screen, some juice gushed from his mouth, but he was still choking and trying to breathe. I kept running with Jeff in my arms to the duplex next door. His face was red, and he was still trying to breathe. My neighbor helped me reach medical services on base by phone. Dr. Sweet told me to turn him upside down and whack his back. I was shaking badly and worried about Jeff's lack of oxygen, but he began breathing a little, though lethargic from the ordeal. The eternity of panic and fear combined did not allow me to recall the time that passed, but the cry to God, though imperfect, was heard and answered. Maybe that was when I began an earnest lifelong interest in every form of prayer.

Six months later, I borrowed downhill skiing clothes and traveled with Don and a friend who encouraged us to try skiing at King's Hill. It was a carefully planned day away from home and baby Jeff. Skiing was hilariously fun, and although I didn't try anything too risky or steep, my legs were snow plowing quite well, if slowly. The second time I skied, I found out the hard way that I was too slow. While in a snow plow on the "dope slope," laughing at take-off and maneuvering maybe fifty feet, my right leg did not move as my body did, and a sound of cracking traveled from my leg to my brain and ears. It was the sound of bones breaking and snapping. My arms began to wave to anyone nearby as the happy day gave way to painful helplessness. The injury sled came, loaded me, covered me, and pulled me into a shed to attach an air splint onto my leg. There were lots of "cliffs" immediately ahead—getting back into Great Falls, my borrowed clothing that would be eventually cut off, a stay in the hospital until I could manage to lift the heavy plaster cast off the floor, not to mention the pain that kept me focusing across the room so I would not pass out, and most of all, a baby son seven months old who was not walking yet.

At the same time this was happening, Jeffrey had developed severe diarrhea. We needed help! My mother, not a veteran airplane flyer, agreed to come. She was needed. When she left, church friends brought meals, and later an "angel," Elaine, came each day to care for Jeffrey and me.

Pictures show that Jeff took his first steps on his first birthday, ahead of me. I was still in a full leg cast. The Fanettes, Parks, and Shepherds came for birthday number one to share the Snoopy cake I managed to make while leaning on crutches. Jeff put his elbow in the air beside his ear and performed steps to the delight of everyone. He also delighted us with his first drum solo as he tried out a drum given him by Bob Park. So the hollowness of the empty beige military house happily broke its silence.

Color and decorating became a thing for me about that time. There was the olive green and blue couch, the dark olive bound rug, the yellow in the kitchen, the gold in the bedroom, and of course the white curtains I made, trimmed in pink and blue rickrack for baby's room. I painted a rocking chair. I antiqued an older upright piano and bookshelf that were given to us and, at a craft class, made some glass olive grapes. I used everything given us.

We joined First Southern Baptist church, located on the corner of 3000 and 9th Ave. South where we enjoyed the small mostly military congregation. We went to work. We continued singing together with a small choir and taught junior high schoolers. I led Girl's Auxiliary, played the piano, scrubbed floors, enjoyed potlucks and showers, and played dominos. I also joined the other base gals who were pregnant at the same time to discuss the next stages of almost everything.

Don was ordained as a deacon in a meaningful ceremony at First Southern. About this time, he tried hunting big game, riding his bike to the dental office, tearing a lawn mower apart in the basement, and helping a friend put a new transmission in a jeep, the alias, "Blue Goose." I prepared and ate wild game for the first time. We both were learning a lot.

Before our time in the US Air Force ended, we were seeking the Lord for answers to where we were to go next. Don had not taken the

Montana State Dental Board so he could not practice in Montana. His mother was ill, and we felt a pull to be nearer to family. The decision was confusing mostly because of the church family and friendships we had made in Montana. A part of us felt very sad to leave the Montana adventure, never to return. I couldn't stop crying the Sunday at church when we announced that our time at Malmstrom was ending. It was just as difficult to see the Anaconda smoke stack through tears in my eyes as we left Great Falls and headed east on highway 87 toward Billings. I watched the famous refinery landmark until it was out of sight.

We thought we would go toward Missouri and en route catch a Mission Conference in Glorieta, New Mexico. Many missionaries were to speak, and we determined to be in prayer before our next step after the military. To my surprise, the stay at the famous retreat campgrounds was fairly unremarkable. I had hoped that God would call us jointly into missions at this conference that gathered missionaries from around the world. My heart was about to burst with the mission possibilities, and I was hoping that Don was also feeling something of interest too. It was a miserable time. He did not. My dream of being called to foreign missions was stuffed somewhere inside.

So on to my parents in Springfield, Missouri, we journeyed. Jeff was a cute eighteen-month-old, and the months we lived there seemed more like a visit as Don began to check out the places in Missouri needing a dentist. Time dragged by as we looked at and considered Springfield, Lebanon, and then El Dorado Springs eighty miles away as potential places to establish a dental practice. We were adapting to a new culture again and missed Montana but accepted the offer of Dr. William Neale to join him in his practice in a town of about 3200 people, El Dorado Springs. Our tireless talk of the great Northwest and military seemed irrelevant to most we met, but one couple in El Dorado Springs talked as we did about their time spent in Germany. That was Dr. Bill and Jan Neale, who thankfully made the transition a lot better.

Neither Don or I felt wholehearted about accepting the opportunity to practice in El Dorado Springs, but Don had spoken with an older retiring dentist, and yes, we were told that this town could support two dentists. Eighty miles was closer to my parents than the previous 1500 miles had been, and Don's mother was still recovering from breast cancer in St. Louis. Our wings of independence were being clipped a bit, but we were eager to be settled with an income. So the teal colored stucco rental on Main Street would be home until we got acquainted and could afford to think about a house. Don rolled paint over the flowered wallpapered walls as I lay on a webbed patio lounge chair in the dining room whose carpet also had big flowers. I was suffering and weak from an attack of colitis. Jeff rode his red tricycle around me in the empty flowered room.

The sun was shining the day the moving van pulled up to the teal stucco four-room rental with bath and kitchen. I was still limping across the lawn because of the broken leg. The town was interested in us it seemed because they would later mention items they saw being moved from the moving van into the house. Welcome to Midwest small town-itis.

New town, new church, and just down the street, new nursery and some fine people to know, but *not exactly what I had planned. How could He now?*

*Rented Home in El Dorado Springs, Missouri*

*Green House Number One, 1969*

# Chapter 9

## STUCCO RENTAL TO GREEN HOUSE #1

While Jeff played on the front porch at 709 Main Street Eldorado Springs, Missouri, we waited for one or both sets of grandparents. We all lived in the same state for the first time. Our rent was $75.00 a month. The commitment was made with Dr. Neale that Don would join his practice just up the street. The rental was temporary, Don assured me. The military housing we left was luxurious by comparison.

From our bed, we listened to the shuffle of something in the attic at night. Little bits of material filtered from the small seams in the ceiling tile. After talking to several local folks including the landlord, it seemed most likely that squirrels had moved in ahead of us. A plan was set in motion to open the attic outside vents and coax the critters out, or something like that.

Then there was the sulfur-smelling water that made filling the bathtub a threat to any good olfactory nerves when the faucet was on, especially for baths. We just opened the windows and waved violently for a while and bought a water softener very soon to help out.

We weren't alone because that smell was a true El Dorado Springs characteristic known by all who lived there.

Fall and winter turned to spring, and I planted my first garden in the backyard down the back steps below the screened porch where Don installed our washer and dryer. Jeff played nearby and helped dig or played in the small yellow plastic swimming pool.

Because our church home was just a few blocks down the street, I could walk to women's missionary or other meetings. We were slowly getting acquainted. We sang some duets at church, and Jeff was settling into the church nursery. We kept our ears open for any available house for sale because at this point, we were hoping to announce that we would have another baby.

It was nearly a year later when we made an offer on a house, a green split level with an unfinished basement and an upstairs in big time need of TLC. We bought Green House #1 for $16,000, and the loan payment was $106 monthly. We were able to begin some improvements while still in the rental house. We worked hard. We chose celery-colored carpeting to go with our blue and avocado couch. We refinished the kitchen cabinets by antiquing them, and I situated a wedding gift of yellow plastic canisters on the cabinet and sewed daisies on the kitchen curtains to match. I was sickened by the remodel smells and paint because, yes, I was pregnant as hoped. This time, we knew the conception signs well before a doctor's confirmation. We felt very blessed.

In Green House #1, Jeff had a room next to ours, and the small guest room across the hall would welcome the new baby in late December. We all shared the same bathroom, which now had a tiny white potty chair where we read books, ate cereal, and praised all the success that came—eventually.

Jeff was a dear. He had some scary asthma attacks during that time though. We would have to get some epinephrine in him so he could breathe. I do not like to recall the gasping sounds of his breathing and pleas for help. If he had a virus with fever, it often would start up his asthma tendencies even in later years. Otherwise, he was a healthy strong boy with still the biggest blue eyes ever. Mrs. Wright, a next-door neighbor, liked spoiling him with daily treats, and Ms. Judy and Marla—our neighbors—took turns doing the same.

Don was busy with golfing, softball, and basketball and was adding a new interest, bird hunting. Queenie, the black and white gentle-souled bird dog, came to live in the dog house in the back to help Don with bird hunting endeavors. We still had Greta, the cockapoo, until her sad end, possibly poisoned by neighbors. We cried together when she was gone, our first pet.

Our church life in El Dorado Springs was filled with some very dear relationships mostly because we began a weekly prayer time in our home, which later went to other homes too. We invited Jesus to be there, knew He was and felt His presence, and talked just to Him, confirming the prayers on each heart by subjects. In other words, we did not pray long prayers that covered everything but short back and forth prayers until we felt that we had released the matter into our lovely Lord's hands. We grew in intimacy with Jesus and each other. Our pastor and his wife joined in, and the time spent there each week sometimes extended to fellowship at someone's house Sunday night after church. All the kids played, and we talked, ate, and headed toward a new week together. Sometimes, I began Sunday dinner preparations on Saturday, and we invited someone over after church. That happened regularly. Linda and Dick, Evelyn and Charley, Pete and Ravina, O. L. and Kay made ten, plus adding any visitors, neighbors, or friends who were always welcome. We grew in fellowship, faith, and in an awareness of a loving Father who answered prayer.

Meanwhile, Don's work at the office was barely doing what we needed financially. He saw the emergencies and not as much restorative dentistry as he needed to grow his part of the practice there. God provided so many times for us though. There were some food gifts from out of nowhere that I still remember. We were content. This second expected baby kept us hopeful and trusting.

After the birth of Jeff on the military base in Great Falls and the complicated recovery, I opted for general anesthesia for this baby. That plan was comfortably in place in early discussions with the doctor. Nevertheless, I was totally miserable, tired, and huge! My doctor was eighteen miles away in Nevada. Traveling to visit my parents in

Springfield soon ended, and my right leg was like a heavy immoveable log when trying to get into a car. With one son already, we of course hoped for a girl, but knowing the gender ahead was not an option in 1969. So when Don said, "We have a *nice big* [9 lbs 14 three-fourths oz] *healthy boy!*" I dissolved into tears. It was either the relief of a safe birth complete or the fact that we didn't get our girl. The codeine made me hallucinate, and I think I went directly into postpartum depression. Just seeing Jason Grant Spurgeon at every feeding was the highlight of every two hours in the hospital. One look at him and never a thought about a girl again. His face was so fat that he had a wrinkle separating line beside his cheek and ear. He had a bit of jaundice, and they found a blood factor because I was O negative, and he was O also. After testing, all was fine. We came home on Christmas day, 1969.

Jason's birth, December 22, 2:00 a.m., came suddenly. Earlier that evening, Jeff had sat on what lap I had left to listen to the church choir sing a beautiful Christmas cantata. Don was in the choir singing, and there were songs about Mary and giving birth, and the melodies rang so in my mind that I felt like a real kindred soul with Mary, intermingling this marvelous Christmas event with our own baby boy event.

With two small children, things changed. *Is this sibling rivalry?* I pondered. No way around it when a new baby who practically filled the infant carrier seat joined Jeffrey's world, family dynamics adjusted. Jeff stood far away in the room while I held Jason, and my heart broke. I was sure that the books had diagnosed it correctly as sibling rivalry. *Is Jeff experiencing feelings of rejection from Jason and me?* I am happy it did not last, Dr. Spock.

"Here, take this baby. He is your son too!" I said as I handed Jason to Don as he lay in bed one Saturday. Don was, in my opinion, comfortable with Jeff and knew he needed extra time, and I felt left out and decided he was leaving Jason out too. Those are the needy thoughts of messed up distorted hormones: irrational, real, and so confusing in relationships. This was a confusion settled by our commitment to each other and asking for God's help. We stumbled around in those corridors more than once and for many years while

I studied and learned more about the physical and hormonal symptoms that phase in and out in a woman's life, specifically mine.

In those baby days, I began journaling and committed myself to a quiet time after a conference on prayer led by our former pastor Bill Little. I journaled about the books I read, the prayers I prayed, people's needs, and my needs. I would do this when the boys napped in the afternoon, and I would sometimes fall asleep surrounded by the diapers I was folding. It was a listening-growing time with the Lord. I sometimes wondered about my life as I sat on the stairs of the split level greenhouse looking out.

*Is this what it is, my life? God's plan?* I questioned.

One day, I sorrowfully wrote in my journal until I filled the whole page with the same sentence. I wrote, "I will never be a foreign missionary. I will never be a foreign missionary. I will never be a foreign missionary," as I hoped for closure to this unforgotten dream and commitment I made when I was young. I cried, and the tears fell on the page as I put the realization on paper over and over until the entire journal page was full. "I will never be a foreign missionary."

Our income in El Dorado Springs wasn't so great, making it evident that we would need to consider something else financially in our lives. Thoughts of a move meant that Green House #1 was all but a beautiful memory with the red flowering cannas that surrounded the concrete block patio where several birthdays were celebrated and a place where a loving mother, Verna Marie Spurgeon was lost to us just six weeks before Jason Grant was born. But we would live there for almost two more years. Jason would eat sand and share Queenie's dog food; Jeff would swing and ride his Sears plastic motorcycle on wheels and play with Phillip. I would grow a huge tomato vine that traveled up the back stairway sending praises to the Missouri sun and humidity. Ordinary.

After Don made the trip to Montana to take the Montana State Dental Board and on his return, he said with great disappointment, "I could not have passed that board. My gold foil fell out in my hand." He said it grimly with shock and disbelief. The board was administered on the grounds of Eastern Montana College in Billings using old army field units in a less than ideal situation for such. By now, I was saying, "But I do not want to go back to Montana." My heart was torn, and another move so far away from family did not seem right to me. However, while Don was taking the board exam, I just happened to attend a women's retreat at Windermere Camp. While there, I totally allowed God to change my heart, and I agreed to go wherever we were led, Montana included. I was so relieved after that decision I had made. But now to hear Don's discouraging words about his doubts on passing the state board, I was confused. The prayer group covered us with much prayer in those days about God's will and this possible move. About a week after his return, the mail came, and in it was a single white post card saying that Don had passed the Montana State Dental Board Exam and now could be licensed to practice there. We couldn't believe it! This was our answer!

Now came one of the most difficult things to do: tell our families.

We decided to just investigate places in Montana first. Jeff was four, and Jason was eighteen months old when we decided to leave them with neighbors, load our 64 Biscayne Chevrolet, drive to Montana, and look for a place to practice and a house. Possibly, we could leave the car there and fly back if all these pieces of the puzzle fit together.

We traveled to Montana to check things out in the hot summer of 1971. While traveling in one of the Dakotas, I had a very severe headache. I buried my face in a pillow. I took some Tylenol and partially slept and prayed. It was then that I had a never to-be-repeated experience. The Lord spoke to me. He said, *Think of the boys in joy. They are happy"* and followed it with, *"You will know it when you see it."* At the very same moment, I was staring in my mind at a brown beige tile flooring in an unknown room, someplace. At almost the same time, my headache was gone, as in completely gone! I was slightly afraid to share what I had seen and heard with Don as we were driving except that my headache was gone. But, I really could not keep the picture and words back either. I told him. Neither of us said much about it, but when we began to look at rental spaces in Great Falls several days later, Don would say, "Is this it?" referring to my vision. We would do a slight chuckle as I shook my head and said a positive, "No! It may be close in some ways but, No!" It was the last day we had to look. We met a contractor, Dick Olson, at 2311 10th Ave. South who had a sign in the window offering the building space for rent. At that time, the space housed a karate studio. I knew the same location had been a hair salon when we lived on the base several years earlier. When we went in the front reception area, we saw a bright red shag carpet on the floor. Our eyes had begun to quickly look at the floors for clues for direction. We then walked into a large mirrored area and looked down. "That's it!" I said with sureness and shock. I had no doubts. The space definitely did not look like a dental office, but the exact color of tile I had seen in my vision as we traveled from Missouri to Montana was right before us.

That evening, we drew plans, picked colors, and decided on a house we had seen in Valley View only once. We drove to Billings and ordered equipment from S.S. White. We charged thousands of dollars of dental equipment there. Our house at 1337 Ave. C, N.W. was purchased for $28,000, with us paying $500.00 up front, and our house in Eldorado Springs would test our faith for another eleven months before selling.

A new chapter started. Was this really another green house?

*Little Travelers*

*Jeffrey Alt Holding Jason Grant*

# Chapter 10

## DARING MOVE BUT NOT TO JAPAN

It was October of 1971 during a beautiful fall season in Missouri. My parents stood on the driveway pavement, tearfully waving as we slowly pulled the twenty-four-foot U-Haul truck down their street and away from 2230 N. Link in Springfield. We had lived in a town seventy miles north, El Dorado Springs, Missouri, for over three years after leaving the big sky of Montana and our time at Malmstrom Air Force Base in Great Falls.

Plan #1 was to tow our white 1966 Chevrolet sedan behind the orange U-Haul truck and all ride together. But the Chevy would not tow. Instead, it crow-hopped on our trial drive. Plan #2 developed out of necessity. When our friends in El Do helped load us, we found we needed to rent an eight-foot trailer also. I would drive the Chevy. We would take a young woman friend in El Dorado, Judy Gerster, who had loved our boys and babysat often. She would help me drive the car and care for Jason who was twenty-two months old. Then we would fly her back home to Missouri. Jason, we thought, would play and sleep in the back seat as we traveled the 1500 miles. Our white vinyl playpen with all the blue balls stamped on it was flattened, placed, and stabilized behind the driver and passenger seats for Jason. Jeff who was an agreeable four-year-old would ride in the *big truck* with his Daddy Don. The little boys with matching coats and their twenty-eight and twenty-nine-year-old parents departed for the long trip, leaving behind grandparents, the state of their births, educations, and growing up memories.

Don's mother had died of breast cancer just two years prior, on November 11, 1969. Jason was not born at that time. Jeff saw his grandmother but was too young to remember her except for a special visit when she was hospitalized one of several times and was able to visit with the three of us in the hospital waiting room. Her joy with this grandchild was quite obvious, even in her weakened condition. It seemed to me we were leaving behind Mom, as I called her, another memory. Verna Marie is buried at the City Cemetery in Owensville, Missouri, south and west of St. Louis where Don was born and raised. Mom's last years were consumed with her fear of the cancer and pain she suffered. She and Dad spent extended times with us in El Dorado Springs as a type of therapy for her and some relief for Don's Dad, Adrian. Her care and fears occupied all the moments we were together and the family found it hard to cope. In those days, Jeff was a toddler so we tried to focus on him for a lighter mood as he rode his first tricycle around the dining room on the flowered carpet.

One day, I remember Mom dropped a milk carton she was getting from the refrigerator. "Crying over spilt milk" was a fact, not a saying, as Mom began to cry about her worthlessness. Not knowing how to handle the emotion, I left the house for a while and ran to a friend's house. I am thankful to this day for that friend, whose name I no longer remember.

Mom was fifty-seven at the time of her death. I did not get to attend the funeral service because Jason was expected. I remember well how the Lord comforted me in the little things. A pastor and wife took Jeff and me to dinner although I could hardly get in and out of their car. My heart was a jumble of emotions on the day of her funeral. I had written a letter to her that Don was able to read to her before her death. It confirmed our love. I had made some pumpkin pies from my garden pumpkin, and I sent those along, making me feel a part, somewhat. Her death left us with a great loss. She definitely had a devoted love for Don, Jeffrey, and me that we knew we would miss.

Dad, in his extreme loneliness, found himself comforted by one of Mom's cousins who lived in Kansas. Her name was Laura Sewell. Laura was admired by all the family for taking care of her invalid husband for years. Walter had been bedridden, needing continual care before his death. Dad married Laura in 1971, the same year as our move. They lived in Kansas, so we were leaving the closest of family in the Midwest. In spite of leaving family, go we did, on the great adventure north. We totally believed and still believe that God led us and had a reason beyond our understanding for the cross-country move.

On the daring trip, we did not have cell phones or walk-ie-talkies. I could run red lights easily, if it meant not losing that orange U-Haul truck from my sight. Jason, sensing the unexpected, did not sleep in the back seat *at all* as we had hoped. We had to stop frequently to get him out of the small space between the playpen and car door where he seemed to slide with great ease. Our first official stop was Topeka, Kansas. The second night on the road we stopped in Ogalala, Nebraska; the third, Buffalo, Wyoming, followed by a long day and into Great Falls. The truck was governed about fifty-five miles per hour, so travel was steady but super slow in the mountains.

When we got to Great Falls, we stopped at the little church on Thirtieth Street we attended while in the military. It was Sunday night, and the evening service was just over. Our older friends, the Fanettes, took our weary little caravan to their house, and we slept in their base-ment for several nights until we could unload into the Valley View house at 1337 Ave. C. Northwest, our address for the next eighteen years.

"I don't think I would have the guts to do now what we did then," Don said in hindsight.

"I wonder," I replied. "Except that step-by-step and as we prayed, we did have peace, but no income of course!" I added.

The house in El Dorado Springs, Missouri, our past home, had not been sold. We had just borrowed $20,000 for dental equipment at a Billings company, and the house in Great Falls we purchased for $28,000 was not available yet. The remodeling of the space for the dental office in Great Falls was costing $10,000. We had no income.

*1337 Avenue C, N.W., Great Falls, Montana*

# Chapter 11

## LIFE IN GREEN HOUSE #2, FAMILY MISSION

We waved good-bye to Don from the east kitchen door. Down the concrete steps, across the concrete patio and burgundy-colored rock wall, he disappeared into the single-car garage. His office was open now, and he was going to work. The space remodeled for his office that once was a beauty shop, then a karate studio, now proudly became his dental office on January 4, 1972. *Would he have any patients?* We wondered. Our advertising consisted of one little ad placed in the local *Tribune* newspaper and word of mouth to our friends. In spite of the circumstances, our faith in the Lord and confirmations surrounding this move gave us almost a supernatural faith and assurance that all would be okay.

We gratefully prayed. We received each patient as God's gift. I prayed daily that Don would be an amazing and kind doctor of dental surgery, sensitive to people and their needs. That was his personal nature already, but I prayed it just the same. God gifted us with Gloria, fresh from dental assisting school, who became both dental assistant and receptionist and a lifelong friend. We attended her dental assistant's graduation ceremony where the new graduates wore beautiful crisp white uniforms.

Life for Don followed a pattern and routine of commitment to provide for a four-year-old Jeffrey Alt, barely two-year-old Jason Grant, and me. Like many stay-at-home moms, I was just busy. I often slid to the floor or collapsed on the back steps around 4:00 p.m. each day, wondering if I would revive by the time Don came home for supper.

I had transportation now. We had the used white Chevy given to us by Don's father while we were in Eldorado Springs and the Chevy Biscayne. The trips I made with the boys were usually to the Western Warehouse on Smelter Avenue where they rode and played on a large flat cart as I marked canned foods and salvaged grocery items to buy. We sometimes went to the Yellow Front store, which later was Anthonys, in the Westgate mall, all on the Northwest side of town. Buttrey's grocery store in Westgate Mall was the place where Jason, at about five, decided to "pick up" some gum on our way out. Seeing the gum when we got home sent us right back to the grocery store to apologize to the store manager. Jason still recalls this humiliating trip. That was all the punishment he needed. He was very sorry. It may have been a good lesson on stealing for all of us.

When I did venture to the Western Warehouse grocery outlet to stock up, it could be a half day challenge. There were a few bribes and threats when the boys tired of the whole ordeal, hid among the boxes, or ran from aisle to aisle, teasing each other. So on the way home, I would often start preparing them by saying, "You get ten points for help with the groceries!" I tried to say this in my happy and opportunistic voice. Don and I had developed a point system monitoring jobs and attitudes, something I read about in a parenting book by Charlie Shed. The points were recorded on a chart I made that was placed on the avocado refrigerator. Points equaled money so that they earned money, usually a nickel or dime, by completing a task. We did this instead of giving an allowance. Brushing teeth, making their bed, or no towels on the floor all had point values either with a plus or minus, which would turn into money or deductions of points. Sometimes, if one was noticeably behind with their points,

I would say, "Ten points to take out this trash" or suggest carrying wood or sweeping. They had great attitudes. I was sorry when they outgrew the point system. At one time, they saved toward jackets that they bought at Big Bear Sporting Goods store in downtown Great Falls. That was a huge purchase of close to $50 each. Jeff's coat was gold, navy, and red. Jason's was two tones of blue, his favorite color. I feel some wisps of guilt now about them buying with their own money what we knew they needed. I'm not sure why.

Growing up on Avenue C meant a basketball hoop on the side of the garage roof and the skateboard ramp built on the down slope of the driveway. It meant learning to ride bikes in a circle on the small patio because of the street hill, the bees each year in the horse-chestnut tree, the swing set, the corner sandbox, the neighbors playing in the playhouse above the garage, the tadpoles carried in buckets from the hill, and the big salamanders residing in our window wells surfacing to show their yellow and black stripes in the summer. There was the special distinctive call in our neighborhood, a two-hand whistle to signal the boys home. Don's handy self-taught whistle brings attention even today. There was Ralph, Chalk, and Gigi, the neighborhood dogs. Our own cockapoo, Ginger, rolled and rooted favorite rocks down the steep front yard only to retrieve them, run them back up the hill, and beg us to throw it again.

There were many Sears Rough Rider jeans that went through the unending wash. I baked cookies, cakes, and pies every week and somehow had time to can green beans, pickles, tomatoes and freeze corn or experiment with the latest recipe that was going around. Quiche was new to us. Taco John's on Sunday night was a favorite. One of the most-liked menus was real Chinese food, thanks to several classes I took from my Chinese friend, Lily Ackert in her home and later in her downtown business. Each week, our family ate three new Chinese dishes as I replicated what I had learned in the last class. Some recipes remain favorites such as beef and peppers, cashew chicken, pan fried fish, wonton soup, and fried rice.

The Valley View kids, Scott Salo, Warren and Shelly Beatty, Jamie Lepard, Lisa, Julie and Dawn McLeod, Lawrence and Kelly Martin, and others would knock at the door regularly. Parents called to check occasionally. Each summer was the best, especially if the temperature reached eighty degrees, signaling a chance to go swimming. I can hear me saying, "It's too cold to go swimming," or "Don't go on the hill where I cannot see you!"

Hill 57 was a very steep hill just east and across the street from our house. One day, I became a really upset mother. The boys toted a BB gun up the hill, and it was this mother—me—who was out of control, upset, and fearful. All returned safely, but it was a story that needed retelling when Don got home. Don always told me, "Get them in position before you spank or swat them. Then you will be in control of your own emotions. Lay them across the sofa arm or your lap." That helped me because often it was back talk or something from their little mouths that triggered my temptation to swing or slap. I'm glad I had a wise husband because I was immediately sorry on any occasion, if I reached out in anger and popped them.

We did spank though. There was a Ping-Pong paddle on top of the refrigerator that was not there for threats or show. I valued the advice of a pastor in Eldorado Springs who said, "When asked by a child for something, a parent's answer should usually be yes except where safety is a concern." Another axiom we used to encourage honesty was this statement: "You will never be punished by us, if you tell the truth."

More parenting advice came from a neighbor who noticed once that Jeff was whining when asking for juice. "Just ignore the request if they whine, until they ask with a normal voice." It worked for us. A spanking was reserved for willful disobedience. I'm so glad those days are over. I think there may be other more successful discipline options depending on the personality of the child and the offense. Forgiveness and reconciliation should always be the final step of the discipline, not a strong feature in this mother.

One day, March 27, 1980 in Green #2, we awoke to a strange sight in the sky and on the ground. Everything was finely covered with gray-white. It was not snow. The sky had turned gray, and the sun could not shine through. It looked like a cold winter day. It was eerie and mysterious outside. We were just discovering this atmospheric phenomenon when the phone rang. Pam, one of Don's assistants, called to see if she was to come to work. Two states west, six hundred miles away, towered a mountain in the Cascade Mountain range called Mount St. Helens. She became volcanic, spewing ash that trailed to the East for hundreds of miles. We were in that path, and the unknowns were just that. How would that fine dust-like powder affect a car's intake system? Should we wear masks to protect our lungs, or even go outside?

The boys put on masks, and we all stepped out onto our black-stained deck now turned white. The boys wrote their names in the super fine ash and darted back into the house. The skies were gray all day. The sun was dulled to a muted glow. Almost everyone who lived in the northwestern United States easily recall where they were and the scenes around them on that day. We were at the corner of Avenue C and Valley View Drive in green house #2.

Everyone remembers another significant event in Great Fall's history. The Anaconda Copper Company's Smelter in Black Eagle closed in 1980. That closure changed the whole economy of Great Falls. Just two years later, it was decided by the EPA, or whoever decides such, that the smokestack, reaching six hundred feet into the air, land marking every corner of the city, should be demolished. The smokestack could be seen for miles when coming into Great Falls or leaving. In 1971 when we moved back, I often watched the smoke-stack from Jason's window as the smoke curled out of it and the sun shone in different patterns on it. I painted numerous pictures of it as did others. Years before, I had cried as I looked back at it when we left Great Falls headed for Missouri. It was a sad and emotional day when people lined the south side of the Missouri River and stood in reverent silence. At the second attempt, the stack crumbled into a mighty pile of bricks. We watched. Some of the used bricks on the outside of our house, which was built later, came from that strong and suppliant image.

As a mother and homemaker, my circles were small, stretching across the Missouri River at times for doctor's visits at the Great Falls Clinic on Central Avenue's one thousand block or a trip to The Paris, later called The Bon, department store downtown. A visit to Rainbow Christian Supply supplied me with study materials, gifts, and books. Just going there seemed to feed and comfort me. When I think of being at home to answer the boys each day when they came in from school calling, "Mom, I'm home," I feel extremely grateful and privileged. The rule was to come straight home to check in before making after-school plans. They were great about this.

Growing pains and life chronicled in #2 Green House are documented in our hearts. *How can eighteen years be so brief?* I thought while remembering all those jeans I washed, the homework, the warm fireplace and earth stove, food, and grandparent visits, driver's licenses, trucks, baseball, soccer, football and basketball, church, small groups, and music ever changing as each of us did. Real and ordinary life.

# Chapter 12

## CHURCH LIFE AND MORE

When we moved back to Montana, we asked each other, "Where are we going to go to church?" We were both considering this early on. This was our second time to move to Great Falls into the pioneer mission's area of the Southern Baptist Convention. There were three choices. First Southern had been our home church while stationed in the military at Malmstrom. How we loved the E.K. Shepherds, Ernest, and wife Johnnie, the pastor and wife there. Don told harrowing stories of moving them from Broomfield, Colorado, during a winter snowstorm. Johnnie said she felt as if they were crossing the Red Sea because the snow along the highway was so high. They were an older couple who nurtured their people unforgettably. There was also Highland Baptist near the base and Westside Baptist, the smallest and nearest to us geographically, to consider. Part of our decision to return to Montana was that we wanted to serve and be used purposefully in our Christian lives.

It seemed that Westside had the greatest needs. They met in a garage converted to a meeting place for the sanctuary. There were folding chairs instead of pews and a congregation of under fifty on a well-attended Sunday. Many who came to church were picked up by a beat-up older model red van owned by the church. It made two trips to areas around Great Falls each Sunday. Since we lived only a few blocks away, we joined the congregation in the little white church within a month of our move. Jason was most unhappy and had a dose of the normal separation anxiety that accompanies many two-year-olds. So one of us stayed in the nursery (living room of a nearby house) with him and about four or five other children during church. There were Dianna and Crystal Jones, Dean and Darcy Osgood, and later, Stephen and Timothy all from two families. We stacked red cardboard blocks, changed diapers, and kept peace until Jason grew into the next class. He joined Jeff in the basement of the house that was turned into makeshift Sunday school classrooms. By that time, I was teaching adults each Sunday, sometimes alternating with Lee Offerdahl.

One Sunday, we studied the scripture about foot washing in John's Gospel. Lee led us into a lively discussion of the pros although Baptists did not practice it as a church ordinance. Teaching was good for me because it made me study more. I took that class very seriously and prepared for hours each week, a little each day and most of Saturday as I pulled the lesson together. I used several versions of the Bible, along with the suggestions from the denomination quarterly with new material every three months. Many were topical studies versus taking any one book of the Bible to study. By now, my Bibles became marked and soft on the edges with use.

During those years as before, I continued to read, fold clothes, sometimes fall asleep, write in a journal, and pray sometime during the day. The church was close, so we attended every function Sunday morning and evening, Wednesday children's groups, and committees for the envisioned new building. Don served on the deacon board, drove the church van, and on Wednesday worked with Royal Ambassadors. We had a growing love and concern for the people he picked up each week in the red van. Some were from very dysfunctional families, and some were very poor. One man, Gerald White—a quiet loner—rarely spoke. We never heard his story, but he was always there waiting, ready for his ride to church and back in the van. Don had Jeff, Jason, and friends in Royal Ambassadors, and at the same time, I continued my love of missions with the teenage girls in a group called Acteens. These four to six girls were in our home regularly for ethnic meals and Sunday afternoon mission outings to Hill 57, which was a well-known needy group of shack-dwellers over the hill from us. The girls led an afternoon Sunday school class for the children living there.

Friends like the Chapmans, the Rogers with MamMaw and Frank Love, the Kisers, the Jones, the Ingrams, the Osgoods, the Carrolls, the Sheasbys, Martins, Pastor Lou and Mary Belcher, and all the kids Don picked up still reappear in our lives and thoughts, never forgotten. When we had a visitor at church, we went to see them within the week. Many returned and stayed. We were whole-hearted in devotion and service. We came to Montana knowing that God's plan was beyond the dental practice or location, but according to His use and purpose in our lives. We embraced the service role and sought it.

One Sunday, when I was not feeling well and did not go to church, Don and Jason came home from church with important things to tell me. Jason had gone to the front during the closing invitation and asked to be baptized. He had wanted to be saved when he was five years old, and we had prayed with him, but now he wanted to follow the Lord in baptism. Jeff had already made a similar commitment and been one of the first baptized in the new baptistry at Westside Baptist Church. "Lord Jesus, I know I have done some things wrong. Please come into my heart!" Don had been talking to the boy's group on Wednesday evenings about repentance and salvation, using those quoted words, and we would hear the boys repeat them at home.

As a family, school, sports, and church blended into the "come and go" stage of life. Hot dogs and macaroni and cheese for supper using paper plates happened more often. We sometimes ate pizza and or Taco Johns on Sunday night, but for the most part, we always had breakfast together and four out of seven evening meals. Eating out was a luxury and costly, so we did not do that too often.

"I'll take Jeff to soccer, and you take Jason to baseball," we would agree. This lasted until they both were driving, approximately ten years from age seven to sixteen with Jeff driving vehicles two and half years before Jason. There was baseball, soccer, basketball, track, BMX biking, add football, and, for a short time, piano. As teenagers, they attended youth group and choir at church.

One busy night, we were on our way to a Meadow Gold League basketball game at North Junior High. The boys were in the backseat. It was still daylight, and we were in the 1966 white Chevy sedan. We were waiting to make a left turn off Smelter when suddenly we were hit from behind, hard, breaking and plummeting the front seats back onto the back seats and the boys. Miraculously, we were not seriously injured although shaken. The evening was a blur to me; the game went on. The driver of the other car had no insurance or license to drive. Our car was totaled, and our necks could hardly move off our pillows for days. The only recourse was to pray that others would not be victims of the same scenario, especially from this illegal driver who had hit us. It amazed me that the game went on, as in life.

But the games were fun. There was the talk with other moms like me. We shared the hopes of a win as well as watching the skills developing through the player's hard work. We watched with pride. Both boys excelled. Jeff was better in basketball, and Jason, in football. They attended camps and made good friends. They still were able to attend church and camps with us. There was little scheduling conflict on Wednesday or Sunday nights in the 1970s and '80s. Respect was given to the importance of church and church-related activities so that rarely, if any, school events were scheduled on Wednesdays or Sundays.

As a young man, Jeff was a skateboard enthusiast and practiced to perfection. The boys always needed new "trucks" and wheels for their boards. Don made the first skateboards out of oak for each of the boys. We stained and varnished them carefully. They were the perfect shape, or so we thought. The planning and anticipation in working together on this project was evident. Jeff chose the word *Alva* to be on his board, and Jason had *WOW* cut from the black sandpaper attached to the boards. Disappointment came when the board did not want to flex. A variety of other boards followed. Then Jeff showed us a drawing of a skateboard ramp from one of his skateboard magazines. There ensued a mighty campaign about the where and how we could manage a ramp in our driveway. The blueprint arrived in the mail and the excitement grew. The ramp was built. On the very first day of use, a neighbor boy, Bobbie, fell and broke his arm. We wondered if this great huge quarter pipe ramp would survive. From that accident, all the kids had to give us written permission from their parents to use the ramp. Both Jeff and Jason went to the top, turned in air and balanced for the downward ride back to earth. Each went on to compete in several local competitions and win some trophies.

After the wind caught the ramp and repositioned it into the neighbor's yard, Don placed a big chain looped to a telephone pole around it to keep it in place and give it a little more time. That also was about the time of the BMX dirt bike interest. I remember those bikes well. Each boy saved money to help buy them. Disappointedly, on two different occasions, the bikes were stolen. What a heartbreaking moment to realize that something so special was forfeited to a thief. Later, Jeff's new stereo system in his old GMC pickup was torn from the truck while it sat right in front of our house. Jeff had worked at Godfather's pizza to purchase the sound system. It was easy to teach about the consequences of stealing when we found ourselves victims. Our 1964 Chevy was also stolen and later recovered.

More life in Green #2 came in the springtime of 1980 when Stopper was born. This little colt had a white blaze, perky step, and inquisitive disposition. He was the son of his mother, Sugar, and his father was Elmer Kicks, a quarter horse. On the morning of his birth, Dr. Bill Rogers, our veterinarian friend called to say the foal was coming. We left the house right away. Our family began announcing his birth and ownership for Jason, who was then about ten. Stopper lives on in 2013, and although his hearing is gone and his back sways, he surely must recall all the attention his owner gave him. Sometimes as a colt, he came for a visit in our Valley View backyard to play. He liked to take Jason's hat off and even wear it (with Jason's help). He enjoyed the water from the hose and careful grooming before carrying Jason back toward the small rented pasture about a half mile away. Jason broke Stopper to ride and trained him to cantor inside the round pen at the Radovich stable west of town. I was there in the dusty and sunny evenings watching a happy young man with noticeable natural abilities as he trained his horse Stopper.

The girls began to call our house. Proms and pictures followed. But hunting every fall with Don was "a must," even if it meant missing school a couple of days or being taken out to the Sieben Livestock Ranch to meet up with the hunters later in the week. This tradition began about 1973 long before they were old enough to take the hunter's safety class. It took weeks of preparation for seven days of hunting. The trip, planned for the second week of November, has become a tradition over the last forty-two years. The smell of deer and elk, the hanging animals to be cut up or divided among the hunters, the hides to be tanned and guns sited before and cleaned well afterward along with the long underwear, orange vests, and the blood of success loaded into the washing machine were just a part of a world, now mine. For many years, we borrowed a meat grinder, set it up in the garage, mixed some beef suet or hamburger with the elk, packaged it, and had meat leftover at the end of the year to share. Stories tumble from the hunters each year of the near-misses or rodeo experiences or food at hunting camp. Participants proudly enjoy this living legacy, even in deep snow or severe temps.

We painted Green house # 2 a couple of times before it got new steel siding. The siding wasn't vertical this time. It was horizontal and had more blue tones in the green, but green, nonetheless. It was a wonderful house and housed many groups, visiting friends and relatives, and Bill. One summer, our guest book recorded fifty-four days of overnight company. Everyone was eager to see Montana.

We seemed to function quite nicely in that house. I loved it. I loved the new addition that was finished one Christmas, and we celebrated it with an open house. We honored our contractor and any others who would come. The back of the house moved out several feet as did the kitchen. By summer, Don found a humongous used air conditioner to install that nearly swept everything off the kitchen counter when turned on. It was so loud that it had us shouting to be heard. But we were cool. We repainted the catsup-stained ceiling over the bar. One time, the catsup seemed to explode from the container as Jeff forcefully set it down and all our heads followed the catsup to the ceiling in one single movement. We replaced the carpeting under the counter that was used as the handiest hand wipe by two little boys. That incident happened at the same eating bar where Algebra was pounded out from the annals of the mysterious into a passing grade.

Do you remember Bill? His is a whole chapter to remember. He was a regular visitor at Green House #2. He could be called a "mission in the air."

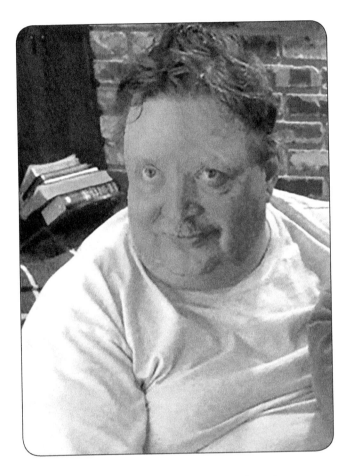

*Bill Sekura, our Canadian friend*

# Chapter 13

## MISSION IN THE AIR

"Sir," the flight attendant said to him, "what is your seat number?" I watched as the slightly hunched round man with navy blue slick jacket boarded the plane. He was large. He struggled to be seated in the row ahead of me. It was difficult enough for him to get into the not-too-roomy seats. *Now he is to move?* I thought while I observed the scene. He scuffled to the aisle, back to my row, and, yes, across my legs to the window seat next to me.

"I'm sorry," he said with a half-embarrassed giggling stammer as the airplane door shut, and our late night flight from Denver began.

His head appeared unusually large as it twitched and jerked. His movements seemed unsure, and when he glanced my way, his eyes seem to roll and rove to the right. "Where had I been?" he asked, catching me by surprise at the early conversation when I was wishing to be ignored.

Above the noise of the 737 engine, I replied, "My father suffered a heart attack in Missouri, and I am returning to my husband and boys in Great Falls."

Not a seasoned traveler myself, I felt cautious about talking with this stranger and being alone. I was hesitant and reserved with the developing situation as I anticipated the two and a half hour flight we would share together. He was genuinely concerned about my father's health and eager to introduce himself as, Bill. He had visited an aunt in the States, the visit being a pleasant reprieve filled with wonderment at how people lived in Kansas.

Bill was called Billy in Tabor, Alberta, Canada, where he lived. He also was known as a hopeless town drunk. His stepfather encouraged him to drink at a very early age while shouting at him over and over, "You'll never amount to anything!" He feared the drunken rages of this man who would kick him against the wall with his pointed cowboy boots beginning at a very young age. As the now-darkened plane moved across the winter sky, Bill described to me those boots and the corner where he crouched.

As he spoke, he leaned in, his head still doing the nervous jerk from his neck, his hands often covering his mouth. Curiously, I began to feel safe and deeply empathetic toward this young man who was treated so badly from an early age. He had not known his biological father; his mother suffered from mental illness and feared defending her son against the attacks of her husband. Bill cared for his mother but felt unloved by both. We spoke of God and Bill's understanding of God as helper and friend. He was a candidate for hope, but he was unsure how to answer the questions of alcohol and abuse in his life.

A few weeks later, "Hi, how are you?" came the distinctly dull monotoned voice over the phone. Always the same sound, it was unmistakably, Bill.

"I have a ride to Great Falls. May I visit?" he asked.

Bill came. He met our boys whom he greatly admired but also envied. At first, the boys were agreeable to our new houseguest's visits, but later, as they grew older, they hesitated when told, "Bill is coming." They knew he was special in many ways and defensively honest to the core so that his childlike heart and social handicaps could embarrass or challenge. He had to learn how to be teased by my husband about saying, "Aye?" (pronounced AAAAA) the common response in Canada for asking a question and to which my husband would always respond, "B?" Basketball competitions outside were serious business, if Bill participated.

During his visits, picking him up at the bus station, going to K-Mart to shop, meeting his friends who brought him, or introducing him to our friends became an interesting joy to me. Yet at the same time, I tried to balance that joy with the feelings of my family who knew our house would not smell quite the same when he left. At this time, Bill was living with his brother, also alcoholic, where good hygiene habits were not a priority. We habitually offered to wash all his clothes, give fresh soap, and a new toothbrush each time he came, which was about three times a year.

The phone rang. "Do you know a Bill Sekura from Tabor, Alberta?" the officer asked.

The Sweetgrass entrance on the Canadian border usually had questions about Bill if he traveled by bus. We came to expect a phone call from the border patrol. To Bill's embarrassment, the officers would empty the entire bus of passengers while they checked him out.

"Yes, we know him. Yes, he is visiting us in Great Falls. Yes, we've known him since 1976. Please do not delay him further," I plead.

There were times I called the border ahead and explained his suspicious look but harmless person. I wanted to shout into the phone, "Just ask him an important date or a score of a Canadian hockey game, or about the United State's political scene or a current president." Bill watched the news about the states, and his memory was excellent.

Meanwhile, sunny changes were happening in spite of long conversations about wanting to marry or the complicated relationships surrounding him. Bill started attending Alcoholics Anonymous. He did not miss for years. We celebrated every year of sobriety with him. We knelt and prayed together in our living room beside the green and blue long couch. Bill announced that October of 1976 became his second birthday; it was a spiritual birthday and new beginning, not forgotten to this day.

We visited Bill in Canada twice; first, while he was able to work for the city garbage service and once for his marriage to Penny. His nervous habits and giggles remain, but we speak of him with honor. After nearly thirty-five years of sobriety, new teeth, new wife, and new life, there is cause. He remembers the days when he did not know if he had one shoe on or no shoes at all when heading for the bar. We are still a phone call away and remain enriched by this real "beauty from ashes" story that Bill's life and friendship represents.

*Calvary Community Church*

*"The three crosses represent the brotherhood of man and woman
In their common dilemma of sin and need,
Linked together,
Touching the forgiveness and covering of,
The Cross of Christ."*

# Chapter 14

## HIS LOVE KNOWS NO CHURCH BOUNDS

The period in church history known as the Charismatic Renewal was just around the corner and at the door of our spiritual journey in the early 1970s. Prayer groups in our home were a common occurrence everywhere we lived since the '60s starting first at Christ Memorial Church with the Rosalind Rinker book *Prayer, Conversing with God*. Talking to Jesus in prayer became personal, and group prayer, dynamic as real as if Jesus were right in the room. We were speaking to Him, not making a speech for one another. We were constantly assured of His great love. God had blessed us and others in these weekly gatherings. Our friends brought their kids, and we either paid a sitter or, most of the time, just let them play in the basement. We knew the person of the Holy Spirit in our lives from Salvation, *as Paraclete*, "one who comes alongside." What I had not experienced was the Holy Spirit in worship. "Forget about yourself and concentrate on Him," was what the worship leader said at Women's Aglow Fellowship. We sang those exact words in a lovely song each time I attended. At Aglow, we were encouraged to sing unto somebody, forget about ourselves, and focus on Jesus.

That was new to me. The hymns I knew were all about Jesus, the Holy Spirit, God, His love, creation, commitment, devotion, faith, and more; however, the added emphasis here seemed to be only on Him whose name, whose presence, whose love and reality came so close it was thick with divinity and spiritual food. My voice blended with others who adored Him as I. Stanzas and page numbers were forgotten. Sometimes, the singing would drift into a united sound of melodies in perfect harmony. I studied about the Holy Spirit. Was there more of Him than I knew? I read all the scriptures, talked with friends, and let my spirit enjoy the revelations that I was receiving almost daily in scriptures, television, or with friends. The same thing was happening across denominational lines. The Catholic Church hosted some of the first spirit-filled groups. The Holy Spirit was an active part of my salvation, and I knew I had already experienced His personhood through acts in my life. There did seem to be more though, and I wanted it all.

I had felt His presence since salvation at nearly nine years of age and even before. So when the 1970s brought a pronounced outpouring around the world, I was a skeptic with others too. My church taught *against* the baptism of the Holy Spirit with the evidence of speaking in tongues and that the dispensation of the other gifts of the spirit in the New Testament was relegated to another Bible time, not for now. However, I was in this time now, and what I learned in Bible study, books, Christian friends, and experience left me desiring everything God had to give me, the *Something More* that Catherine Marshall wrote about in her book titled the same.

I understood that the gifts empowered our service to the Body of Christ and released a fresh joy and trust. I read *Nine O'clock in the Morning* by Dennis Bennett and Merlin Carouther's books *Prison to Praise* and then *Power in Praise*.

One Saturday, while my hair was in rollers and I sat drying my hair under the noisy table model hair dryer with its cap covering my head, I read something that stopped me with truth. It said something like: "Receiving the Holy Spirit is much like receiving Christ in your heart—you believe by faith as you did at Salvation." That was easy. *I can do that*, I inwardly voiced to myself. *I can do that, so I will, right now. How easy could that be?* So I said in my heart, *Lord, I receive all you have for me, the fullness of the Holy Spirit experienced in Acts or anything that is a gift from You.* In other words, I surrendered and believed as I did at salvation.

Nothing dramatic happened until weeks later. I lay down with Jason on his bed before his nap in the upstairs east bedroom, then got up and started down the stairs. Some strange sounds I had never heard came into my mind. They were, "Aw ve pu nae chu la," and I could say them over and over. I repeated the sounds, thinking I would not remember them but of course can vocalize them to this day. I have listened for those sounds in various languages and believe I will hear them and know their real meaning someday. The rhythm and flow of a language unlearned now flows easily, a gift opened and used in prayer and ministry. It comes easily and is perfect for certain times and moments, unselfish and from the Holy Spirit unlike my generally self-motivated words and life. The words seem lifted up as a pure prayer or a means to be empty of my doing as I stand planless before a God I honor with my lips as I do my heart. Yes, it did appear I was experiencing the gift of tongues given to the believers in Acts 2, taught, and reinforced in the epistles by Paul.

The same thing happened to at least seven or eight more friends at approximately the same time. Don experienced the same later as he rode up the ski lift at King's Hill. Several women were now praying over their husbands and families and agreeing with others, while our fairly new pastor vehemently pronounced from the pulpit that this movement, specifically tongues, was demonic.

Our church, Westside Baptist in Great Falls, was building a new church building. We were highly involved. We vowed not to cause division over doctrine. Word was out, however, and we were suspect. How could we be an enemy in the denomination of our upbringing where we labored with others with singleness of heart since our own new birth at salvation and throughout our marriage? It was not an easy time as we bottled our new joy with silence while quietly feasting on the richness of His word and, yes, this new experience. Some Baptists finally accepted the word "renewal," but it was increasingly obvious that lines were drawn, leaving us no choice but to end our membership at this church we loved. We didn't know what to do or where to go. How could we be so joyous and fugitives at the same time?

In those days, mainline denominations were all facing this outpouring with questions. Even the words, spiritual renewal offended some who vocally preached against all such, saying the gifts ended with the New Testament and were not from God but from the devil himself. The choice to remove ourselves from Southern Baptists was naturally misunderstood and confusing to our mostly Baptist family. For months, we had our own worship service at home. We sang. The boys took turns taking the offering. We had communion. We sought answers not knowing where we should go to worship with others corporately. One Sunday, I remember crying for fellowship. The TV didn't "do" it although several ministries greatly fed me. Some other friends who had departed the denomination long before us were attending Great Falls Christian Fellowship on Sunday evenings at the Ursuline Center. They invited us. We visited and heard teachings there about the whole body of Christ not just one denomination. We loved it and continued. The boys took their Bibles, met with the adults, and learned to find scriptures on their own. There was singing and wonderful worship unto Him and fellowship weekly. In the summer, we attended camps at the C Bar N Campground on the Dearborn River near Augusta. Scriptures in the Old Testament became exciting and alive, linked to Jesus. There was no membership, just awesome joyful praise and worship. Many songs were sung from the Bible. We met people from many church denominations in town who attended and joined them happily without dissension.

Eventually, the Fellowship began an after-school Bible class for the children in a home on a weekday, and I was in a weekly intercession prayer group with several others. The group prayed following the guidance of Georgia Penniman, a teacher on prayer from Youth With A Mission who taught at special conferences. As we prayed, we first quietly opened our hearts to the Lord to confess our sins for cleansing, then took authority over the enemy in Jesus's name, then asked for a new filling of the Holy Spirit, and lastly, we asked the Lord what He wanted us to see or pray out that day. We listened and wrote, then shared and prayed. Those prayer times were amazing. The leadership at the Fellowship asked us to take notes so that they could review. We wanted to have a "covering" and so submitted agreeably.

We became a part of a home group that met weekly, quite often in our home. Many were water baptized in the azure blue waters of the Dearborn River. Our boys were prayed for at camp, asking for the baptism of the Holy Spirit. We were together as a family, singing, praising, rejoicing, and learning. It was a refreshing time but also tragically a time when various religious cults appeared such as the one Jim Jones led in Ghana, where hundreds followed their leader to death. Our families questioned us with understandable concern. I prayed that they, too, could experience the baptism of the Holy Spirit.

It was subtle, and although we felt alert to any false or erring teachings, over time and with heavy hearts, we saw the Christian fellowship move toward something called shepherding. As in the first church, everyone in the church "had all things in common." Eventually, everyone had a "shepherd" over them. That shepherd was consulted on such things as buying a house. He also collected the tithe. The home groups originally for teaching and fellowship seemed now a place of control and accountability we did not submit to. Women were devalued in ministry, and we felt the youth and our boys at this important stage needed acceptance and church-based guidance and fellowship. We counseled with a Great Falls Christian Fellowship pastor who dismissed us from the Christian Fellowship, if we were unable to follow the shepherding of those over us. I still recall the sadness and heavy-hearted feeling and release at the same time as we walked from that home into the evening sunlight, realizing a remarkable time in our lives was giving way to an unknown. For the second time in our lives, we were churchless. It was very troubling and easy to still remember. We ran to Jesus, our friend, and it seemed He already had us in mind.

The boys had friends in many churches in Great Falls, but Calvary Community had a youth pastor, and the boys were invited to go with their group to a youth camp. This became the first of many events that followed for them, including a traveling youth choir. That youth ministry helped us "find our way." Calvary was an interdenominational church. Most of the leadership had Assembly of God ties.

Love seemed to run down the aisles at Calvary and embrace us. We served and worshipped there for over ten years and loved it. We ministered in music and taught third grade Sunday school. I led and organized the first women's ministry where Bible studies and prayer groups met weekly. Our family attended almost everything and served however we were needed. Don was asked to be an elder. It was a happy glorious time. Some seasoned Christians from around the city with many denominational backgrounds worshipped there as well. The music and worship were blessed. Renae made the piano sound as if it had millions of keys playing all at once. The cantatas and dramas involved the whole congregation.

The vision to use music beyond the walls of the building became a reality. Great Falls Civic Center seating over 1700 people staged the gospel message in song, costumes, and lavish settings each Easter and Christmas. Thousands attended the many performances and outreaches.

The church building did not have a cross on the outside, so I designed and arranged with a welding expert to create a three cross roughened steel sculpture, which still stands outside the present Victory Church. The Lord impressed me with an understanding of the linked and touching crosses. The plaque reads: "The three crosses represent the brotherhood of man and woman in their common dilemma of sin and need, linked together touching the forgiveness and covering of the Cross of Christ."

Sadly, our gifted spiritual leader, pastor, and friend was unable to accept accountability to those over him. Rejecting the counsel of his elders, he chose not to look at his weakness or take a sabbatical toward healing. Instead, when asked to leave, he began a new church only to repeat the same dangerous scenarios further destroying the trust of those who followed his leadership. A gapping ugly cancer in many followers is still being healed to this day. Others traveled courageously on, seeking fellowship in the Body of Christ elsewhere.

We became reluctant travelers as well, not wishing to go to another church but in some ways, completing a circle when we returned to the denominational covering and oversight of the "organized church" at Central Assembly of God.

The transition seemed slow in coming, but some of the classes taught there helped. John Wilkinson's Sunday School class and after that the changing classes every three months with a variety of subjects and teachers helped us meet people and connect. Even the gray hair of Pastor Warneke in the pulpit helped us experience security after what we had just been through. We sang together and joined the choir. Our home was open as usual for missionaries or groups or small groups called Share groups, then Care groups. Don served as a deacon, then elder, at various times. I taught studies for women and led Heart 2 Heart, a mentoring program matching one woman with another. I was asked to be at the helm of a struggling women's ministry. I had been there before and loved seeing women relate and find a place of service and growth. Every experience was fulfilling. There were monthly board meetings, planning meetings, prayer meetings, Bible study meetings, retreats, and special events to direct. Each event took much time and planning.

Women's Ministry invited Georgia Penniman for a Prayer Conference, then the author Jo Anna Weaver and singer Negleatha Johnson came for special women's retreats. Other speakers were housed, workshops and leaders accommodated, and each event sponsored by the women's board was covered by a prayer team. Women who did not know each other before became friends and laborers together. There were no computers or e-mail contacts for organizational expediency. Everything was by dial-up telephone or in person, over lunch. These events were planned by all, and the Body of Christ was working together using each part for the whole as in Corinthians. Following the legacy of the Women's Christmas Dinner, my responsibility included overseeing that event. At least one hundred women, coordinated by committees, were enlisted to serve in some way. This was a glamorous event because the women made it so, each decorating a table to serve guests with their own tableware and creativity for centerpieces. Up to four hundred women attended, often crowding into the foyer and extending into the ministry center of the church. The special speakers and twinkling Christmas lights, the men servers, and catered meals seemed blessed by God. This event, appreciated by women in the local church and beyond, brought God's love and grace across denominational borders again.

"What a fellowship, what a joy divine, leaning on the everlasting arms," words from the hymn embodies all the lives we have known in Christ's body, His church. We jokingly have said, "We know everybody in town because we have gone to so many churches." We are thankful that we love all we have fellowshipped with and delight to see them always, our brothers and sisters in Christ . . . the Church with no boundaries.

# Chapter 15

## I BELIEVE YOU ARE MY HEALER

"You must stay in this dark room," Mother said.

That was the advice for anyone in 1946 who had scarlet fever or red measles, and in my case, both at the same time. I was very young but remembered being in that dark room with just a little light showing across the room, sneaking in from the sides of the blinds. We were still in the brown asphalt house in Strafford. The only doctor near was the one who delivered me, Dr. Focht. He was highly respected and made house calls.

I don't remember being a sickly child, just the usual scars garnishing both legs or knees from the merry-go-round in the school playground. When I was a little older and in the white house, I had a high fever requiring a doctor to drive from Springfield to check on me.

The Whooping cough "caught" me before the days of immunization. Dickie Hopper, who was a bit younger than I, had it at the same time. I recalled we had a whooping not-so-good time while our parents visited one Sunday. With whooping cough, you cough and cough until you throw up. What bonding Dickie and I experienced that Sunday afternoon.

One summer, my skin and whites in my eyes turned yellow due to jaundice. It was thought to be very contagious and required a long period of rest. I had a lighter case, they said, but the quarantine of many weeks seemed very long to me.

A few health issues occurred when Don and I married in 1964, making that first summer in St. Louis unpleasant. I was a new bride who anticipated nervously her first teaching experience. I was to teach English at Ritenour Senior High School, one of the largest schools in St. Louis. The size alone was scary. So perhaps I was just anxious. I didn't think that life away from family affected me too much. For whatever reason, my colon did not like the situation, and irritable bowel and associated symptoms were diagnosed. Those symptoms decided to follow me everywhere, especially when we made a move, or I experienced inner conflict or did not digest properly.

My health, life, and energy seemed adequate until an unknown hit my body in early May 1974. I was thirty-two. I developed a type of viral pneumonia, which left me unable to function as I had previously. The boys were four and six with Jeff in kindergarten.

One day, I remember trying to clean and wax a hardwood floor in the upstairs bedrooms where the boys slept. The sun was shining in Jason's window to the East. On that day, the work I was doing was just too much. I could not breathe as before. Another time I recall trying to go to church while struggling just to move from the foyer, holding to the rail as I moved down the steps. I had to quit teaching the adult Sunday school class. I began to "monitorize" my life with thoughts such as, *Can I make it?* measuring endurance for anything other than the very basics of life in our household.

One time, a caring friend, Latrelle Chapman, came to the back door unexpectedly. She came to vacuum and clean. She had been in the hospital in traction some time before my illness and remembered my visits and food and a similar gesture toward her. Her kindness toward me felt unnecessary at the time, but I still recall it gratefully. Another neighbor, Gladys Poodry, whom I rarely saw, offered to take me to the doctor. She knew the breathing struggles I had and was sympathetic.

Many times our vacuum cleaner stayed in the hall for days as we stepped over and around it. Don was busily making a living and taking on other responsibilities as I now paced myself. I did not go anywhere, stayed in bed for weeks while thinking the break I longed for would soon come, and I would feel better. If I shopped, I sometimes needed help getting back into the car to recover and breathe.

The Petite Shop downtown on Central, owned by Joyce Nesbit, had lovely clothes. One Saturday, Don took me there. I still remember the difficulty of that moment and the disappointment I felt when I realized I could not stand or shop even for this short time. I struggled back to our car. Events became landmarks of symptoms to get past. One doctor suggested costal chronditis; another, hyperventilation; another stereotyped me as a southern belle and asked me if I did my own housework. That really offended me. I felt misunderstood while being very sick for a very long time.

It was Dr. Eidson who heard the click in my chest indicating a prolapsed mitral valve in my heart, confirmed by imaging tests and often diagnosed in young white slender females. He put me on Inderal, a beta-blocker that I would be on for years. Even with little improvement, Dr. Eidson saw me regularly to see if he still heard the same sound. His eyes would twinkle and his head would nod in rhythm with my heartbeat as he looked away, saying, "It's still there . . . no change. They are working on a medicine to help with this," he would say. That always encouraged me.

"Could I talk to anyone you see with the same thing?" I asked on one visit.

"No, you would not want to do that," he said.

I guess he thought it might magnify the symptoms in my mind. Instead, he offered, "Medicine finds that as one ages and the heart enlarges, the prolapse might improve because the bubbled relaxed *chordae tendineae* are pulled straighter."

Twenty years and I still was not able to begin normal activities. If we traveled, I had to lie down in the back of our station wagon for at least part of the time, always recovering. I remember a trip to Texas and one to Lethbridge. They are miserable memories because I was always trying to recover, get my breath, or not move so I could breathe better.

The life-consuming symptoms remained. I had a list of triggers but no real solutions. One time, I walked up the hill and around the corner to the Moreland's house where we had a kids' Sunday school class after school. It was less than a fourth mile, but I remember sensing some medical event. Sure enough, when I got there, I had to lie down on the living room sofa, and people gathered around me to pray. Vera Buchman was rubbing my arm. I wished inside for her to stop so that I would not use my energy to respond to the touch, just so I could breathe. As usual and about twenty minutes later, I could begin to get a deeper breath, and my eyes would begin to open, and I could think about sitting up but often remained hazy and unsteady.

While at home so much, I read the Bible from beginning to end and also other inspiring books such as everything of Catherine Marshall's *Beyond Ourselves* and *The Holy Spirit and You* and some books by the Sandfords about healing inner memories. I walked back to childhood and invited Christ to enter any place that needed His touch of healing and my trust or forgiveness. My journals record the ministry of many Christian books about varied subjects. Now many versions of the Bible later, I can't stop reading. My goal became to read every version of the Bible I had, and I continue.

I also learned to play the autoharp during that time to fulfill the music urges I could not commit to in real life. I would sit on the end of the bed, strumming chords and singing or work on all the scripture songs that we sang in the '70s. That whole experience was healing in itself. Don and I learned to sing scripture song duets accompanied by the autoharp. I loved to sing those songs with Don. However, the risk of error on the autoharp made me nervous and still does. One discordant strum, and the song was a failure to me. My playing was not very proficient, but the music was an outlet for the prison I felt my life had become. The words filled the air with a needed message of love and hope.

I was in that valley when I heard of a watercolor class for beginners being offered at the YWCA. I wondered if I could make it, physically. I did go, and I loved it and did not mind the teacher's less-than-encouraging remarks as she exclaimed, "No, no, no! Not that way!" She did finally concede that I had guts to try.

Many people prayed for me during those years as I floundered along, hoping each prayer would be the answer and bring healing. My family and friends prayed and believed. Don would sometimes nudge me to go and be prayed for. He believed in total healing and wanted me to feel better. If Jimmy Baker was on TV and said, "Lay hands on yourself or have someone else lay hands on you," I usually did it. I recall a really sweet experience in the basement TV room in #2 green house in Valley View. Jason was about six years old and, encouraged by the speaker on TV, laid his little hand on my chest and prayed for me. I received all those prayers and am still amazed at my life now compared to then. I lived as an invalid, managing maybe one event a day. I used to just be thankful that I got through anything. Those troubling occasions were at the same time, great victories. Some were embarrassing scenes.

Once we were singing in a musical production at Calvary Community Church. We practiced many hours, which was a physical stretch that I planned around carefully. Before a certain performance at Christmas in our green satin dresses made especially for the occasion, we had met to pray in the room behind the auditorium before the concert. I was struggling. I knew I had to lie down in order to recover. Vivid is the picture of me lying on the floor with Gary Hart taking my hand while saying, "Come on, get up!" I knew I was embarrassing everyone else too, but I had to lie flat to recover and give my body a chance. I sang. I looked and felt very weak and never wanted to repeat such a scene again.

In 1981, Don decided we should go to the Mayo clinic in Rochester, Minnesota. There, a heart cauterization angiogram was performed. Consults with more doctors who were not sure what to call these symptoms resulted. I loved the time with Don there, but I received only a suggestion that I should start walking short distances and gain weight. I began to walk. I would walk down Valley View

Drive and continue onto the dusty road leading to Hill 57 in the field, turn around, and come back. I eventually swam regularly at the Natatorium. I wore flippers, goggles, swim hat, and ear plugs to secure me in the water so that I could relax and pace. I was still swimming when we began to build our house in 1987, and to this day, I am still exercising in the water.

We did make one more trip to try to get help at the Prolapse Mitral Valve Center in Birmingham, Alabama. My local doctor mocked the idea. For me, however, it was the beginning of a turnaround after over twenty years. They tested my heart and breathing in many ways, but what I heard from them was that I was not alone. They asked me about symptoms, and I heard myself saying, "Yes," "Yes," "Yes" to their questions. I had not related those symptoms to the havoc in my chest. I heard from them scenarios that fit me exactly. I felt understood: headaches, IBS, fatigue, chest, breathing discomfort, and so many symptoms that fit into a category, which affected the autonomic nervous system. They thought it was a glitch that had occurred in utero, affecting the autonomic nervous system. I had to make a commitment to more medication for at least nine months and then was to return. I had new hope. God used all of it to gradually heal the most chronic and severe incapacitating symptoms. We still do not have a named diagnosis for those years.

Once, while attending Women's Aglow fellowship, I heard a prophecy given specifically to me. It said, "The years the cankerworm has destroyed would be restored to you!" That is referencing Joel 2:25, KJV. I believe now that those years have been restored. I have heart issues but of another kind, which do allow me to function. I am not a slave to inability as I was for so long. I definitely know how to be thankful that I can do what I do each day. I thank God when I remember the continual healing in my life to include irritable bowel syndrome, atrial fibrillation, fibromyalgia, interstitial cystitis, temporal arteritis, broken leg, hysterectomy, hernia repair, and panic attacks. Is God my physician healer?

There is a song we sing called "Healer." Some of the words say:

"I believe You're my healer.
I believe You are all I need. Jesus You're all I need.
I believe You're my fortress.
I believe You're more than enough for me.
Jesus, You're all I need.
Jesus, You're all I need.
Because
Nothing is impossible for You!"

# Chapter 16

## ARTIST, ME?

"Take this big sheet of newsprint paper and tempera paint with you!" said Mrs. McGee. "Our classroom provides the school bulletin board for spring," she finished.

I was six by then. Another student and I were sent out into the school hallway to begin the project. The newsprint was placed on the cold concrete floor. We wondered, *What exactly are we supposed to do?*

The duck was large and very yellow and carried an umbrella. I drew it. We painted it and then cut out the yellow duck with orange bill. There were spring flowers too that would go along the front. Tulips, I believe.

Was it also springtime when I took that first watercolor class in 1977 at the YWCA? That means this story takes a huge leap from grade school, high school, and college with no motivating art interest for thirty years. I drew occasional side view pencil-drawn faces and doodles on school notebooks, and later, I did draw out the complete design of my wedding dress that mother sewed. That was easy. The art majors that I saw in college dressed funny. Abstractions and nonobjective art were laughed at and questioned, "Was it art?" The art most people I knew understood was a picture of a "something" framed and hanging on the wall. I certainly did not know the difference between a print or an original.

In the late 1960s, I went with a friend to an art and craft show in El Dorado Springs, Missouri. Jan Neale was a tole painter. She followed patterns and, with careful brush strokes, painted realistic flowers, leaves, vines, or fruit on wood or metal. I admired her work greatly. I wasn't interested in trying it or knitting or croqueting the items I saw for sale at the bazaar. A rather bright acrylic painting caught my eye. It was painted loosely. I told Don about it first, then went back and bought it, our first piece of original art. It cost twenty-five dollars.

My interest peaked further with the Art in the Park show and sale that the Junior League women's organization in Great Falls sponsored each year in October. Four-by-eight sized sheets of plywood filled the gymnasium's tarp-covered floor to display art from around the state during one weekend. The crowds were large. At first, I wanted Don to go with me, but I soon enjoyed the event alone as I scoured up and down the aisles, looking, touching, memorizing names and the look or style of each artist.

I began buying a few small things from artists, but mostly, I just soaked in the experience, especially the paintings selected by an artist juror to be in a show. They had to be good. There was also a small local art shop downtown Great Falls I often visited, just to look. I loved the watercolors. At that point, neither had I picked up my own pencil or brush, or had I considered doing so.

In the mid-1970s, I signed up for my first class. Frustrated because of my physical limitations I happened to read about classes offered at the YWCA, one being a class for beginning watercolor. I wasn't sure where the "Y" was. Even the supply list was like uncharted territory, and the attendees, total strangers.

My first day, I watched the paper be taped down and some easy painted washes added to paper before being told to go back to our places to try the same. My new workshop vocabulary included water, brushes, paint, color mixing, mats, more colors, and techniques like using salt to separate pigment, tissue to blot out clouds, or a credit card or palette knife to scrape paint away for trees and twigs. A trip to Gibson Park to paint outdoors proved way too overwhelming. The landscape was huge to this novice compared to the small paper in front of me.

At home, the dining room table became my place to practice all the techniques. I had ideas of saving the white paper for the whites in the painting early on, and even in the night as I lay in bed, I strategized the whole painting process with possible subjects. From the dining table I went to the basement guest/toy room to paint. I would lay works in progress on the guest bed and long for someone to tell me what to do next. One day, a friend visited who was a real artist. Suzanne was a member of an art cooperative in Great Falls. I asked her to take a look at what I was doing, and she very graciously showed me the good corner of one painting, not the 95 percent bad. I studied what she saw that was good. I learned from her, that it was a fresh look that reveals the real nature of transparent watercolor, not the overworked areas. I was just enjoying the process of painting at that point with absolutely no intentions of doing something more with what I was painting. My neighbors often stopped by to see what I was painting. They would rave and encourage.

Gladys said, "You should go down to Westgate Mall for the Christmas show and sell some of your paintings!"

The thought of that totally unnerved me. "No, I don't think so," I replied.

It took me another year before I considered it.

My small booth was at the east end of the mall and next to two dear and encouraging women artists, Theola Sederholm and Doris Williams. I don't remember if I sold anything or not, but we all exchanged a small painting among us.

Rainbow Frame Gallery began to do some matting and framing for me on a small scale. They were honest and complimentary. They invited me to have a show in their gallery, in October 1982. Many of our friends came, and several paintings sold! I was not convinced that I was an artist and shied from the title. I knew I had a long way to go in comparison with the artists whose work I admired. However, that was the day I told Don that I had been Dr. Spurgeon's wife all these years, and today, he was Carol Spurgeon's husband!

Gallery 16, a co-op for area fine artists, had a shop on Fifth Street in Great Falls that I frequented. It was a small place with pottery in the window and various types of paintings inside. After workshops with two or three local artists, I asked Gallery 16 to jury my work to show and sell. That began a wonderful learning relationship with the Gallery for which I am most thankful. With each new venture, it seemed I was learning more that I did not know about painting. Each workshop or book I studied made me more inquisitive and determined. Right or wrong, I tried it anyway.

Jean Halverson, a Great Falls watercolorist, greatly influenced me. I nearly drooled over her softened and simple landscapes, her birds, or cattails. When I joined others in a workshop with her, I observed firsthand her fine drawing skills, which were greatly lacking in my background. I took a drawing class at the Y and enjoyed it. After years of observing and practice, my eye does direct my hand more confidently. That class was the first time I realized that I could produce a likeness of a subject.

It is easy to say that I have learned a lot from those whose work I admire. In the early stages, I was eager to learn from anyone who offered a beginner's class. I signed up eagerly. I still learn in workshops. Just for fun, I mention names of workshop artists starting with the beginning ones that I have had: Nan Lovington, Jean Halverson, Robert Kercher, Elliot Eaton, Christopher Shink, Joseph Bohler, Frederick Wong, Mario Cooper, Judi Betts, Ted Nuttall, Frank Francese, Lian Zhan, Joseph Zubukvic, and Tom Francisconi. Many of these three- to five-day workshops inspired me to work harder and, hopefully, bump me into the next level.

I was asked to teach beginners. I took those assignments very seriously spending days of preparation with lesson plans, lectures, and demos packed into the huge navy bag with red trim that transported paints, paper, brushes, and examples to and from the workshop locations. I had some large classes at Paris Gibson Square, Gallery 16, Central Assembly of God church, Montana School for the Deaf and Blind, C.M. Russell Museum, the Demolay Building, Brighten up

Shop, GFAA at Westgate Shopping Mall, The Rainbow Retirement Home, and others.

I've had some nice recognition. Galleries accepted my work to show and sell, but I really aspired to be juried into shows, which would evaluate my progress. I started with Art in the Park locally. I eagerly listened to the jurors, wrote down their comments, and learned about my work and that of others. I kept asking exactly what it was that made certain pieces exceptional. I was now aware of many art forms and could recognize both artist's style and the media they chose. I was learning a lot. Putting it mildly, I became a sponge, absorbing all I could.

Don and I inherited an oriental brushstroke painting of a bird perched on bamboo from his parents. It was small and intriguing to me. The painter was the father of a friend of Don's, Ben Leung of China. Ben was a fellow student at Southwest Baptist University. I believe this painting as well as my interest in Asian culture as a child inspired my early interest in the space, simplicity, and spontaneity paramount in Oriental brushstroke paintings. I began to practice the various steps outlined in brushstroke books. No one instructed me, but a reward of my practice sessions came when I was awarded a first in the watercolor division at the state fair by juror Robert Orduno, whose famed work "The Portage of the Missouri River" graces the Great Falls airport. His huge mural painting is wonderful. He admired mine, bamboo on rice paper, which I have kept as an example of the many oriental brushstroke paintings or studies I enjoy doing.

In 1990, I was invited to join three other artists for a showing at the Montana Governor's Mansion in Helena. I felt quite out of my league but naturally honored as my watercolors joined my mentor Jean Halverson's paintings on the wall together in the Helena show at the governor's mansion.

In 2001, an invitation came from the American Egg Federation to be the Montana artist to paint an egg to represent Montana at the White House in Washington D.C. What a stretch that was! I tried rice paper and glue first then experimented with acrylics. I finally painted directly onto the egg with acrylic paints. Since Montana is known as a large sheep producing state, I painted sheep similar to the ones I had used in a painting. Hands held sheep in three positions. The Montana State flower, the bitterroot, was painted on the top and bottom of the egg. The egg joined other eggs in a beautiful display of talent from around the country. Don and I enjoyed a trip to Washington D.C. for a reception in the White House Rose Garden, where we met Mrs. George W. Bush.

In 2007 The Montana State Fair Board purchased a piece entitled "Belt Creek" to be included in their permanent collection. I was honored. Several one-person shows, awards and juried acceptance have followed. As a learner, I remain surprised at this part of my life. *Was this a part of the "all things" in Romans 8?*

# Chapter 17

## ART, COULD HE?

When Russ Michaels, our music and associate pastor, asked me to produce original paintings for the new foyer in the addition of Central Assembly of God at 2001 Central, I said a quick no followed with, "But I know enough artists that I can help you find someone. I will be happy to do that." Those were my exact words.

One morning, soon after his call to me, I awoke with a type of vision, and scripture on my mind. It was the scripture, Isaiah 53:6: "All we like sheep have gone astray; we have turned everyone to his own way but the Lord has laid on Him the iniquity of us all." That verse was straight from the King James Version that I had memorized around age ten. The picture I saw in my mind was one of the blackness surrounding our need for rescue from a deep dark hole or pit representing the near-death state of our sinful nature. The next picture was one of all those sins that kept us in a place of darkness being carried on the shoulders of Jesus as he embraced the cross. Those struggles of sin and lostness were being redeemed by the love of our Savior according to God's plan for sin payment. They were the sins of the past, present, and even the future. That alone was astounding. As a result, the next picture was one of us, mankind, restored, or held up to be adored because of the work accomplished for us by the cross. What I had in my mind was not a painting of Christ but instead images demonstrating the work of the cross. We were those sheep in Isaiah 53.

I began to draw some very rough sketches, trying to show what I envisioned in my mind—arms reaching for us in a place of darkness, arms or hands carrying all, and then us restored or saved as a result. We were held up with His hands again, now restored and adored. It was at that point that Don and I set up a time to visit our friends the McKameys at their sheep ranch. I had already drawn and painted a few sheep, but on this trip, I wanted to photograph Don holding sheep in specific positions with his hands in a rescuing position as in holding a sheep over a fence, then another with a sheep around his neck, and finally, a lamb that he was holding toward the sky to look at.

"Hurry up," he yelled. "These guys are heavy!"

"Take off your cap, Don. I can't visualize Jesus in that cap!" I yelled back.

It was a sunny day, good for shadows, and one rather friendly lamb complied. The photo session was completed. I now had more resources. When the pictures were developed, I started drawing again. Yes, we were like sheep as the scripture in Isaiah had pointed out. In my mind, the painting was there and just needed to be painted.

I told Pastor Russ, "Yes, I will attempt paintings for the foyer." They needed to be large so after talking to The Brighten Up Shop in downtown Great Falls, they agreed to order some large sheets of watercolor paper from New York. We bought a four-by-eight sheet of plywood needed to mount the paper on before painting began. All the sketches were collecting in my sketchbook, so I could pick the ones I liked right down to individual sheep with different looks. I remember distinctly, taking a big breath while saying, "Here goes," when the time came to start the actual painting. I had already prayed about the outcome, but after the first day, I was awash with a huge sense of failure. When Don came home from work, I told him I had ruined the painting already. He said, "You'll pull it out!" Not my sentiments at all.

The next morning, a group of girl friends came to our house for a prayer gathering. We had prayed as usual. When they were about to leave, Vera said, "How is your painting coming along?" I expressed my disappointment in the first day's "paint to paper" work. She said, "Well, may we see it?" So off to the studio we went where in a short time, the paper, the paint, the brushes, the room, my hands became the objects of sincere and believing prayer.

I painted on, confidently. The painting "Rescued . . . Redeemed . . . Restored," not perfect by any means, has technical insufficiencies in drawing and execution, but the message, heart, and inspiration seem to overtake my inabilities. When the painting, image size 36 x 59 is viewed, the sheep get the attention first, but very quickly, the awesome message of the cross overtakes. For spiritual blinded and resistant eyes, the sheep are enough to see, but to those who care to look further, the piece becomes personal and touches those who are forever thankful for their rescue, redemption, and completed state of restoration. It might be called my signature piece because its purpose and ministry continues on from the comments I am blessed to hear. Nothing pleases me more than the delight on the faces of recipients who know about their own rescue, or to realize that the work of the cross can travel through this painting anywhere it goes.

A few ideas were coming along for the other painting they wanted, but not as clearly as the rescued painting. I kept drawing a less sophisticated, restful, pastoral landscape as a beginning idea. I saw some mountains in a watercolor teaching book showing various species of trees. I really liked the center mountain and labeled it a possibility. I completed a painting study and then a complete paint-ing for trial. One had many trees in it and a lone figure with arms upraised in praise. *No,* I admitted to myself. The yellows did not seem to work.

Pastor Michaels gave me fabric swatches with colors of the future carpet and pews in the new church auditorium. That helped. I began a large landscape with birch trees on each side and a snow scene with a stream through the side to middle, creating some depth. The large burgundy mountain with the white paper working as snow set a stage for something in the middle. Was it for a person?

We received a phone call from someone we hardly knew. The situation described to us brought concern and fear to our hearts. Don left for Missoula because of the urgency we felt. While he was gone, I prayed and read my Bible for direction, peace, and safety for all. The final image for this second painting happened while I was reading the indelible words of Psalm 42. Everything I needed and more was right there. There was the downcast soul, there was the hope and the promise of yet praising Him. I read the Psalm over and over. Then a bonus happened. I also knew what was to go in the center of the painting! It was from Psalm 42, and it was a deer. I kept singing that Psalm, and by the ending verses, I knew about the hope we had in God, in all circumstances.

"As the deer pants for streams of water, so
my soul pants for you, O God.
Why are you cast down oh my soul?
And why are you disquieted within me?
Put your hope in God, for I will yet praise Him,
My Savior and my God." Psalm. 42:1, 5, 11 (NIV)

The deer runs to water when it is hurt or injured. I was running to the hope I knew could sustain us in our crisis. Yes, a deer would go near the middle of the painting along with a cross, central to all we do, laid across, looking like a log. A part of the cross, I lifted out with my brush to recover the white of the paper. There was comfort and hope, and I could praise Him in all things. The deer turned out nicely, and Pastor Warneke, a big game hunter, said, "That is the best you have ever done." Bless him. These two paintings hang in the foyer at Central Assembly of God Church in Great Falls Montana. I donated my time, work, and framing and wrote on the back that they belong to my family if a change happens at the church, and they are no longer needed. Broken Wheel Gallery framed both of them. Their size, 60 inches by 40, require two people to lift, hang, or move.

I never considered having prints made of anything until many people approached me requesting them. Gallery 16 members seemed to look down on prints as a piece of paper, rather worthless; however in this case, the message could affordably go to more people if prints were made.

At this time in 1996, my dear mother was very ill, and I was traveling to Missouri often. While there, I chatted with a printing company, and by 1997, I had my first prints and cards ordered. They arrived by freight on huge flats carefully wrapped in layers of plastic. We prepared a "home" for them upstairs at our house. Don and I carried a few at a time of the two thousand prints of the two paintings. Fearful that even one print might be damaged or creased in the moving process, I was excessively paranoid about these "babies" not knowing that one entire printing was already damaged. I began to sell them to people at church for $50.00 each.

"Do you know there is a flaw in your print?" asked a buyer one Sunday morning. He was right. In my excitement and haste when I signed them off to print, I overlooked the tiny flaw on the lamb's leg, lower left. Warfare began. I had to notify all previous buyers. The company said they could not reprint. It was a very heavy moment of decision. What should I do? By this time, several prints had been damaged in shipping or in one instance, a frame shop glued on a backing improperly. The calls and situations were handled one by one. I could not pay for a reprint from my art account. Was it worth it? When the decision was made to "stomp" ahead, defying the enemy because of the message in the painting, the warfare stopped. In fact, the company paid half the cost on reprinting, and more blessings followed in sales. Comments came to me from all over regarding God's use of the message of "Rescued . . . Redeemed . . . Restored" now hanging in churches or used as a theme in retreats or just giving encouragement to someone who saw themselves redeemed and restored. Because I did have them reprinted, I now have the slightly flawed poster prints to give away to others for mission trips around the world.

Near the fall in 1990, I was approached to create a special painting needed by the Boys and Girls Club and used as a fund raiser.

I was very honored to be considered. I painted "Everybody Needs Somebody," a painting of grandson Jacob with Bozo the clown as one possibility, but the final choice was "Just a Touch," a painting of a little blonde-headed girl curiously examining a pool of running water. The original sold for $950.00 at their benefit auction. I had seventy-five prints of the same given me to sell.

Many paintings are gifted to organizations, benefit auctions, or churches where I feel they are needed or will be appreciated. The joy is really unsought but very real when I see one being viewed or used. I usually have forgotten the gift or, in some cases, the cause I gave to. One such occasion happened when I gave a framed print of "Rescued . . . Redeemed . . . Restored" to Southwest Baptist University in Bolivar, Missouri, where Don and I first met. We visited the campus in Bolivar, also the area of my father's birth where many Davolt's still live. A couple of years after leaving a painting at the college, I received a letter and some correspondence from the alumni director. Then came a letter saying I was nominated and chosen to receive a Life Service Award during homecoming ceremonies of 2000. It was a very humbling thought to me, and I felt undeserving. The Art Department invited me to have a show of my work during the same time. It was a very happy and special time. A few former classmates, Don, my sister Judy and her husband David, plus my elderly father attended the service of recognition. I had been an English major while a student there but came back as an artist still with a heart for missions.

Early on, I gave myself a life challenge regarding my art. I wanted to gain signature membership in a nationally juried show. I still remember my first entries, mostly because they were so bad. The competition comes from very fine artists who enter from all over the United States. The exhibit requirements are very specific and detailed, down to the color of mats. Of course, they must be original, completed within a couple of years, never shown before, and follow guidelines perfectly or be denied acceptance. In the days of sending slides of the pieces entered, if an edge of anything but the painting showed, it would not be considered. I remember well cutting and loading negatives into viewing folders and using Mylar tape to block edges, hoping to be accepted. It did not happen until 1997, with a painting called "Mystical Lady in Mother's Photos." I wanted to kiss the artist juror, Maxine Masterfield. I still feel that way if I meet the challenge of acceptance and pass. Since that time, I have not only been accepted continually, allowing me to place MTWS (Montana Watercolor Society) on my paintings, but also have won several awards given by jurors. Some paintings have sold during the show, which definitely encourages me.

In 2013, the painting "Hunting Camp----Two Feet of Snow" earned acceptance in my first international competition held in San Diego. I smiled for months. Still smiling. How could this happen?

Even with several one person shows to my name, I face an element of failure every time I paint. I must come to terms with it, always. I often delay painting because I doubt my abilities to create the look I have in my heart and mind. I desire the best from me. Yet the process of something inside coming out can be very uplifting too. I think of myself as a self-learning artist with a developing spatial eye, an ever developing eye, for the medium I use. Watercolor painting set a stage for new friendships and challenges beyond anything I could have dreamed.

Painting was mingling with my dreams now. Speaking of dreams, *How could He resurrect a dream? How could He remember a fifty-year-old cry of surrender now? How could He allow me to pray and serve needy ones around the world now? How could He use the art from me to voice a message of redemption? How Could He heal and give me faith that I could serve others through missions at this juncture in my life?*

*"Rescued….Redeemed….Restored" Isaiah: 53:6*

*Psalm 42*

# Chapter 18

## MISSIONS STORY

"I think we should do that." It was Don whispering to me near the end of a presentation at our church. It was 1989. Two rather low-key speaking gentlemen dressed in suits came from Springfield, Missouri to speak to the congregation. They represented HealthCare Ministries. These men were telling about international trips centered in meeting health care and spiritual needs in third world countries. HealthCare Ministries traveled as teams to the neediest countries at the request of appointed missionaries already in a country. They organized the teams and supplies for each trip in Springfield, Missouri, and the team members took the bags of medical inventory needed into countries while limiting their own personal luggage. Usually, a team would include medical doctors, nurses, dentists, optometrists, pharmacists, and other support people.

These men ended their talk with, "If anyone is interested, fill out this white card indicating that interest." That was when Don leaned to me and said, "I think we should do that."

This was more than forty years after I had cried in the basement of Strafford Baptist Church as I struggled with what I knew the Lord wanted of me. I still loved to listen to those involved in missions around the world, and we gave generously to their causes; however, I was no longer as burdened by my call to missions as I had been. Besides that, I was nearing fifty years old. I had buried it. I had to.

*Really?* I thought. Don's comment was interesting, but I doubted inside it would *really* happen. I did not realize at the time how our future would be affected by his statement or by the little card we filled out that morning.

We did become volunteers on record with HealthCare ministries by writing our personal testimony and by providing the several references needed by HealthCare. We sent a small fee that could be applied to a trip, if we went. *Could He?* Don was busy at the office working and saving money for the boys' educations. Jeff was playing basketball at Northwest College in Seattle, and Jason was playing football at Charles M. Russell High School in his senior year. We were also building our first home.

The late eighties moved into the nineties easily without any follow up on that card we had filled out, until 1999, over ten years later when the HealthCare organization called Don one day at the office. The caller told him about an opportunity to go into North Vietnam and do dentistry with a medical team early the following year.

"Would you want to go with me?" he asked when he got home from the office.

"Would you go without me?" I asked.

"I would rather not go without you," he answered.

During those ten years, we had once prepared for a trip to Wuhan China with Operation Blessing's medical ministry. That trip was cancelled because of the lack of safety in China following the American accidental bombing of the Chinese Embassy in Kosovo. To say I was devastated doesn't fit the feeling I had. In fact, no words except extreme disappointment and extreme loss are even close. My chance to go tell on foreign soil was foiled within two days of departure. I grieved. It felt as if I had experienced a death to a dream, once again.

*Vietnam?* Now the question was, having never worked in Don's office, could I go as a support member on the team since I was not medically trained? *What else did God have in mind?* The dental office was not my regular stomping ground. We had several obstacles to consider, including my health, and left the decision to the staff of HealthCare in Springfield to decide our eligibility.

HealthCare took a chance on me and agreed, saying there were many support needs on a team. It did help my qualifications that I had joined Don at the Great Falls Rescue Mission dental clinic as a volunteer dental assistant. He had trained me to follow orders, develop X-rays, provide gauze, scrub and sterilize instruments, and write information on charts. From the start of our time at the mission, we prayed with each patient. For me, that was the best part: Don prayed for the men, and I prayed with the women after asking them about their needs. We were told that if we went to Vietnam, we could not pray or even mention the words *God*, *Jesus*, and *Bible* because that country was communist controlled, and in so doing, we could jeopardize the visas of the resident missionaries.

Sensitive countries require approved visas before entering, so we had extra paperwork to send to Washington as we prepared. HealthCare Ministries recommended a medication called lariam, a wide-spectrum drug used to prevent malaria. We updated our shots and added the specific shots prescribed for Vietnam. We began the lariam well before we left. We were told that common side-effects of that drug included anxiety, panic attacks, or noticeable mood swings.

We were accepted, and we committed to this trip. It sure seemed late in life to be going on a foreign mission's trip. Even more surprising was that I was serving with a medical team because of Don. He was the reason I could go. The wonder of this happening was starting to demonstrate to me God's faithfulness to the little we offer Him. It also meant that God remembered . . . me. That touched me deeply. We both had served in our local church settings wherever we were, but now it was as if the Apostle Paul's heart to purposely go throughout Asia was becoming my heart as we prepared. North Vietnam was the very first trip with HealthCare, and it had all the extras that any "first" should. That would include being out of touch with our families for the entire time as well as not seeing a fork, knife, or spoon for a week. We had some culture shocking events ahead, some of which I recorded in a month-long painting marathon when we returned.

# Extraordinary God

We left a day early to stay overnight in Los Angeles before meeting the team at the international departure flight area. When we got to the airport, our senses were heightened with the sight of so many people going all over the world. We arrived the requested three hours before the departure and nervously met the other team members for the first time. Everything was a new experience. We became a part of long lines, paper documents to show, and luggage to check. Those lines of people were backed up in different directions. We were managing inventory lists, our luggage, questions from the robotic officials behind glassed windows, and our passports with their stamp from the Vietnamese Embassy in Washington D.C., which we were either getting out to show or stuffing safely away. Flying west meant that we would see more night than day for a very long time. We passed the inspection without problems and headed off over the ocean toward the first refueling stop—Osaka, Japan.

I was thrilled out of my mind. Were we really stopping in Japan? Doris Spencer, the career missionary I wrote to as a girl, served there for many years, and my memory of her letters made this stop endearing. Sadly, it was only an hour stop and in the dark of night. We never left the airport, but I did get off the plane and bought some Japanese cracker treats. I was there.

Back in the plane, we started another leg of the long flight. This time, to Bangkok, Thailand. Once again, I could not sleep and felt extremely jittery inside. I tried my best to ignore the familiar symptoms and asked some on the team to pray for me. I could not sit still. Instead, I walked the aisles. The cold hands, irritable colon, and shakiness came swishing into my body along with an inability to concentrate. I was praying desperately and expected relief any time.

Bangkok remains a blur except for a small room we slept in for a few hours, before our next flight to Hanoi. The small room was arranged for us so that the team did not have to clear security again. Our grateful bodies slept a few hours, and I seemed slightly better. Hanoi was still at least five hours away. We were cautioned once again not to draw attention to ourselves and definitely not to say the name of Jesus, God, or mention Bible or church from now on.

Several hours later, we were flying over waving tropical foliage in our descent to the small roughly built white airport building which read "Hanoi" in black letters. It was surrounded by Vietnamese Migs or military airplanes. The officers outside were uniformed and carried guns. It was 2001, and the Vietnam War, which the Vietnamese named the American War, was over, but North Vietnam was controlled by a communist military government. My feet felt good on the ground. We were told to get into the airport building in twos, trying not to look like a group, although our white skin belied us. We were instructed not to talk or speak while leaving the airport and, of course, not to take pictures.

Inside the terminal building was off-limits to the Vietnamese people who stood outside, hoping to see who was getting off the little plane. Our smiling, tall missionary hosts, Nancy and Bob Eberling towered above the sea of relatively short Asian onlookers, all with beautiful straight black hair. We were silently praying that the suitcases would clear security. We sighed with relief and thanksgiving when our prayers were answered. Our luggage was there, and the medical supplies were not confiscated. Once outside the terminal, the team loaded into a small waiting van, pushed through the crowd and onto a busy and narrow roadway in the midst of rice paddies. We were clearly on our way.

At first glance, we began to see the round pointed straw hats of workers in rice fields, motorbikes instead of cars, water buffalo led by children and adults, and bicycles loaded with extra people, chickens, pigs, bamboo, wood, and vegetables. I was overwhelmed by the sensory menagerie. Compared to my world in the US, there were few similarities except the sky and the land. Even the sky was dulled by the smokiness of burning wood.

The clothes hanging off small balconies flashed a bit of color contrast to the buildings made of tin or pieces of wood, grayed by aged mildew or rusty iron. It was obvious that the Vietnamese reused everything, especially the remnants of war, their history recording many. It appeared to me that the storefronts, crowded with wares, had no doors, and that most merchants lived there also. Village ran into village, ethnic women with stone-like curious faces stared at us as we passed. They wore black boxy hats and some had colored striped fabric visible beneath layers of clothing. We were told that these groups of peoples had come from nearby southern China. We watched as the van moved and honked its way through, passing within inches near those walking or cycling this road north. The constant honks were to warn anyone on the road to not move or to keep moving because of our van's proximity to them. Our destination was Cao Bang, near the southern China border. We were told the drive of 180 miles north from Hanoi would take eleven hours. We traveled a couple of hours before stopping to eat.

Stepping around three iron cooking pots on the sidewalk and climbing a small flight of steps, we found ourselves in a plain cloudy gray room, empty except for a few low tables and chairs. The hazed windows reflected a gray dreariness and with little ventilation; the smell, a mixture of wood smoke, and fish sauce.

I was having trouble focusing my eyes on the cans of soda brought to us. I also felt the all-too-familiar swishing sensations passing through my body. I asked for a toilet and was surprised that they did have one although very small. I noticed a couple of mosquitoes floating in the warm stale air. I had tissues in my pocket, a common directive to all team members on any mission trip, and in this case, a humanitarian trip. Because of the government's suspicious stance, the word *mission* could not be used, *humanitarian* only. I had to leave the table again. By now, the sensations were asking me to flee, move, or run, someplace. It was a horrible feeling. Don knew something was wrong and found me.

"Don," I said with urgency. "We have to go home, now!"

In stern disbelief of my ridiculous request, he laid his hand on my shaking shoulder and said, "Carol, we *cannot* go home!" "Well then, please pray for me!" I begged. I felt the comforting weight of his hand on my shoulder again as he prayed. I did not eat but instead thought if I walked, I might shake this *thing*. I walked outside and circled the cooking pots on the sidewalk near the road. I really wanted to run, even on the dangerous dusty road, but prayers were being answered when Dean, a pharmacist on the team, began talking to Don. He recognized the symptoms and offered to help with Xanax used to treat panic attacks. I am forever grateful to a loving Father and these angels of mercy, Dean and Xanax.

Crawling back into the van, the rest of the long bouncing trip north became foggy as my head fell onto Don's leg. I could hear the constant honking of the horns, but the time was melting as my shaking body relaxed, and I slept. It was still daylight when we made another stop, and with tissue in hand, the men went to one side of the road and the women to the other for needed stops before traveling on.

That night, the long trip ended at a hotel in Cao Bong where we unloaded and discovered our net covered low beds, a shower with potty combo in the same small space, and a thin grayed towel to share. There were mostly carts or bicycles on the streets outside, and inside, as I passed a larger meeting room downstairs, I saw chicken bones left strewn on the white tile floor. They remained there for days.

"Tomorrow, we will see the orphanage where we will set up the clinic," announced our team leader, Gary Higgins.

In the early morning while still dark, we heard the footsteps of many people outside. We heard wheels turning on the rough streets and the squeals of pigs. Each morning, the sounds began at 3:00 a.m. of sellers and animals going to the open market to set up. By 6:00

a.m., the loudspeakers shouted several minutes of Vietnamese over the city. We imagined that the message voiced reminders of government allegiance for the new day, but of course, we could not understand the language.

The walk to breakfast took us past small open-to-the-street shops, people selling from the sidewalks, and mostly women balancing huge loads at the ends of a single bamboo pole. They walked gracefully with a steady soft swinging gait to an unheard rhythm. As foreigners, we were wandering by twos, sometimes threes, and did not seem to elicit welcoming or inquisitive faces of those we met. Those passing by remained stoic and focused upon their own immediate tasks. Seldom, maybe twice, I recalled a reserved slight look that recognized or acknowledged our presence as we walked down this street each day. Did we cause fear, or did the culture restrict their openness to strangers? I suspected the later.

Rounding the corner a block or two away, we neared our restaurant destination. Outside and near the door, large bowls of green leafy vegetables were being sorted and washed by women who squatted on the ground. We knew we would not be eating the greens no matter how great they looked because the water was unsafe for us. Not wanting to risk the God-provided opportunity of being there, we observed every precaution. Just inside the door, the women cooking seemed to recognize the Eberlings who began to look over the small counter that held a bowl of boiled eggs, a whole boiled chicken, and a bowl of greens. They pointed toward the open fire pit, speaking in Vietnamese to order Pho, the same breakfast for all eleven of us. Pho is noodles-in-broth with chicken meat and bones chopped together. Tissues on the table were used to wipe pre-used chopsticks. Don's knees rested at least six inches above the four-foot-square low tables. With broth and chopsticks, we tipped our bowls to our lips when needed. At one meal, we had soup served to us with a raw egg staring at us from our soup bowls. When we ate, few of us removed coats or hats because the winter air was very cool.

Perhaps the greatest hardship was not physical or cultural. Our conversations could not contain the very heart of why we were there or the fellowship we shared because of the cross of Christ. That remained an important rule for the seven days there even though a sign at the orphanage entrance read, "Assembly of God Orphanage of Cao Bang." World Missions Outreach provided rice, housing, clothes, and now medical attention for the children who could not be cared for by their families. In most cases, before coming to the orphanage, the children had lived in a single dwelling crowded together with several other families, or they had no one at all to care for them.

In the orphanage, the children had a chance to go to school and get a coat and food. We brought many coats with us along with sunglasses and plastic type shoes. Balloons made into animals by our team leader brought happy smiles. The children had toys of rocks, sticks, chicken feathers, and a type of handmade hacky sack. They used our discarded plastic water bottles as footballs. They lined up for meals with their small plastic chairs in tow. They laughed, played, and washed their own clothes by hand, the oldest ones helping the youngest. What great kids, all with black straight hair and broad happy smiles unless they were too shy. Even those warmed up before the final tearful good-byes were said at the end of the week.

HealthCare teams have goals and schedules warranting certain order about the day, but the orphanage director had an order also. He started us with tea with Ho Chi Minh. I say that because a head-bust of Ho Chi Minh sat on the table in the small room where we gathered for tea before seeing patients. I loved the tea because I could grasp the tiny tea cup with my cold hands for warmth. I feared insulting our host if I did not join him in tea with other team members twice a day. The question remained whether the tea water was boiled sufficiently for safety. I drank it. Don did not.

Our goal was two-fold: love the children in the name of Jesus Christ and pray silently they would know this Jesus who loved them and gave Himself for them. That prayer continues to this day. Secondly, begin medical health records, administer inoculations, vitamins, and worm medicine, give toothbrushes with instructions in dental hygiene, check, clean, and remove teeth as needed. Most medical mission trips take an optician to exam and give out reading and prescription glasses.

I began having songs float through my mind. I longed to sing "Jesus Loves Me" out loud. I said the words on the inside and hummed it on the outside while in North Vietnam. That was a sad barrier. Two of our interpreters, Hian and Hann, clung to us in admiration and knew our love returned, but we could not share the Good News with them. We have, however, been in touch with them through Julie, another team member who returned to Vietnam, learned the language, and stayed for over two years teaching English and sharing in relationships as she could.

After about three days of medication, I was functioning better, adapting and assisting Don every day. I also painted briefly one afternoon as the children gathered around. As much as I was a grateful recipient of God's faithfulness to me regarding my call to missions fifty years prior, by the end of the week, I short-sidedly said to Don, "We don't have to do this again." After a lifetime of desiring to be right there, *How could I . . . say such?*

Vietnam was the first of now-twelve health–care-related trips. God makes each so rewardingly miraculous that as we recover from one trip, we are often thinking about the next one. Financially, each team member pays their own way. Some of the costs can be counted as a contribution. When my dad died in 1998, we put aside enough of his money for five trips. The money is gone now, but God continues to provide.

After returning from Vietnam, I combed through photos and videos frame by frame, hour after hour, rediscovering and experiencing this culture beyond belief. I had one month to produce a scheduled show for Gallery 16. I began to paint and draw day and night.

The title of that show was easy: "A People and Culture . . . Beyond Belief." There were twenty-four paintings in all plus some paintings on rice paper that were matted. One large painting sold as did all the matted ones. They told the story of the people I saw while there. I hoped that Vietnam veterans would come to see the show and experience a type of healing, if it was needed. I received several notes written in a guest book verifying that it was so.

Another show followed another HealthCare Ministries trip, this time, to India. I called the show "India and Iris." We did not see flowers in India or Vietnam, and the Iris showed the many colors and beauty I saw and loved in India, especially in the women's clothing. We saw hungry people who were unemployed because the tea fields had closed down exports of tea. There were no schools, hospitals, or solid infrastructures in and around Kerala in Southern India.

Out of respect, we wore national dress that covered us from head to toe. The weather was extremely hot. Streets were dusty, and cows and chickens roamed at will. The images from which to paint were memories in my head and very vivid. It was easy and a real privilege to get inside all those images and share on paper the contrasts I experienced while there.

"Tug," the elephant portrait showing his friendly eye, befriended me with another print. He was my "working friend" from India whom I photographed from our crowded and hot small van while traveling. I feared our van would touch the huge creature as we passed.

God used other mission trips to inspire paintings as well: Chile, South Africa, Mexico, Peru, and the Philippines. Many more paintings await. There are no lack of ideas or heartfelt subjects, especially when going to these places. My website slogan is "Many subjects and approaches are my best and chosen friends." The needs and opportunities to share this faithful God vary by country. These medical mission trips commit to going to unreached, third world needy places. Believe me, third world is a real term, unlike the poorest of poor we know in the United States. I wish I could take you to the sweltering, makeshift set ups from which we have worked. Our attitudes remain flexible and eager to make it work with God's help, and He does. *How Could He, indeed!*

It is our beloved privilege to ask each person if we can pray with them. We have personally witnessed visible salvation, restoration, healing, and smiles of hope. The response of an older lady in communist-controlled Myanmar still encourages us to fulfill Jesus's commission given in Matthew 28:19–20. This Burmese lady said,

"I am very old.
I am very tired.
I am very poor.
It is good to have some hope."

I have not forgotten the other peoples around the world who have endeared themselves forever to me in an unexplainable bond. I wish I could write about every country: the stories and faces, especially the faces, of the people still in memory and prayer: South Africa (Delft near Cape Town), Chile, India, Philippines, Myanmar (Burma), Africa (Kenya), Mexico (San Luis Potosi and Puerto Vallarta), Peru (Quechua peoples), and Corumba, Brazil. We thank Him that He can and does take the impossibilities we live and attach His faithfulness so that a dream becomes possible.

How could He make a dream come true? And more? How could He remember an eleven-year-old's cry of surrender? How could He allow me to pray and serve needy ones around the world after I had known Him for fifty years? How could He use the art from me to voice a message of redemption? How Could He heal me and give faith that I could go? How could He love me so? The answer is written in a book whose author is called:

*Faithful, Everlasting, True, Merciful, Keeper of Promises, Full of Grace and Abounding in Love toward all men... Indeed He Is.*

"The One who calls you is Faithful He will do it." (1 Thessalonians 5:24, NIV)

*Tug, My Indian Friend*
*Kerala, India*

*Every Day in the Andes*
*Peru*

*"Baby Hungry!" . . . All Over The World*
*as they come up to you and voice "Baby Hungry!"*

*Clinic #6… A Hopeful Wait*
*India*

*"Thank You!"*
*India*

*Morning Seat in Myanmar*

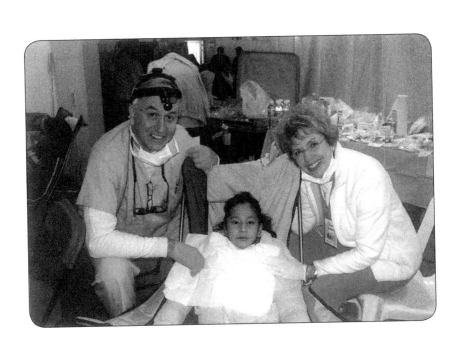

# PART II

## "HE CAN!"

*T*he ordinary journey takes amazing turns for all of us. Adventures become tragedies with no explanations. Or the same situation may quickly turn into a victorious surprise as in "the check didn't come," "the call was too late," or "it happened *just in time* as if purposed so."

When eyes turn heavenward, "the call" or "the check" magically erases disbelief and replaces it with trust and assured relief.

The following ordinaries show a pattern of life, loss, and new life again. They are included here to give courage and strength to the possibilities of "He can!" in Romans 8:28.

Be strong and of good courage. "He can!"

# Chapter 19

## PRAYED FOR, BELIEVED FOR, RELEASED

Tulips were covered with snow on May 15, 1967, sending a chill through my bulging body. I wrapped my arms tightly to myself as we left our home in base housing at 3936A Locust, Great Falls, Montana, for the Malmstrom Air Force hospital. Time was ticking by, yet our clock seemed to stop. It was Monday now.

On Sunday the 14th I had greeted friends at First Southern Baptist church by answering their questions with, "Still two weeks to go!" Pleasantly I thought, *Next year, I will get to stand up as a mother on Mother's Day, but not this ye*ar. Mother's day 1967 would be over in a few hours.

The pink and blue room was ready for either a boy or girl. Scientific ways to determine the sex of a baby before birth were not known at that time. Everyone guessed and was surprised when each baby came. Some made predictions according to pregnancy symptoms. We were prepared with a list of names for both girls and boys but nothing selected for sure. Our friends advised us to look at the baby and say, "This boy is a Gary or a Sam or another Don," by the baby's features, sounds, or movements after birth.

The maternity clothes I had sewn had grown faded and snug. The new and used baby clothes were freshly washed and laid softly in the newly painted white chest with the sprayed pink and blue pull-knobs. Even the wooden rocking chair was painted white and modeled a blue tie-on seat cushion. The borrowed bassinet in our bedroom had a light blue soft material that hung to the floor. I had made the cover and completed it with a white ribbon bow. Were we ready? Our friends in Montana along with family members back in Texas and Missouri were all anticipating this baby with us.

Don was fishing with Bob during the Mother's Day weekend. Even though our due date was over two weeks away, I lay on our bed feeling lonely and somewhat nervous that the Daddy-to-be would not be with me for the birth.

The base hospital was only blocks away so that when my water dribbles turned to occasional gushes sometime after midnight on Mother's day, I woke Don who, as planned, quickly scurried toward the closet and previously packed suitcase as if we had practiced this like a fire drill in our minds many times.

We passed the snowy-covered tulips and got into the same turquoise Chevrolet driven to Montana in August 1966 and drove away. The sky was dark, and the air crisp just like the dark curtained labor room where I lay on a less-than-comfortable cold metal table.

"No, the doctor isn't here yet," she answered as the faceless attendant left.

Don sat in a chair beside me as the ripping pushing pain intensified. There had been no birthing classes or discussions about what to do or expect during labor and delivery. The screaming woman I couldn't see in another curtained slot convinced me I would not scream.

The delivery doctor gave Don permission to be present for the birth. But before Dr. Doucet finally arrived, Don saw the baby's dark hair. The unborn referred to as *it* became "It is a boy!" And I heard the baby cry. The nurses dashed away with him too soon. While the stitching was going on, I was warned to lie flat. After births at that time, those having a spinal epidural had to lie flat for six hours to prevent severe headaches. Those hours were forever! My bed was a lonely island. Don went back to work. No one came. At last, this baby boy swaddled tightly in a blanket visited his mama. I looked into his tiny face. Being afraid to unswaddle him, I held him close for a brief unbelieving moment but soon took the risk of laying him before me on the bed and unwinding the receiving blanket. I saw his hands and feet. He had a little hat on too. *Should I take it off?* I pondered alone. He weighed 7lbs 12oz and was 21 1/2 inches long. His daddy Don called him the most beautiful baby in the world. During the 1960s, only a few new mothers chose to breastfeed their babies, but I was so happy to experience motherhood that I didn't want to miss this part. However, my breast's hurt with growing fullness and all the scrubbing, salve, and steps to nursing were frustrating. I sweat. *"Can I do this?"* I asked the older short round bouncy nurse. Her reply was most encouraging to me. While speeding away, she said, "Honey, all it takes is a nipple!" I was reassured.

We studied the list of names again together going over them repeatedly. Of course, this boy's middle name would be Alt from his father and grandfather's middle name. Don gave the final nod to Jeffrey. Even the mention of the word brings out maternal and nurturing instinctive feelings. This baby was prayed for, believed for, and released to God before his conception.

Parenting became to me a series of blundering moves in a wilderness rescued only by God's love, grace, and mercy. As a growing perfectionist, I was so responsible. I wish I could "smell the roses" again, laugh, and play pat-a-cake. The happy photos of Jeff dressed in cute hats and coats for outings help me forget being drenched in breast milk in my green Sunday dress, embarrassed.

"Why am I embarrassed?" I ask now. Thinking of the growing strong and healthy boy is a better thought. When Jeffrey Alt was 5 months old, I flew to Missouri to visit my mother and dad. I recall how the airplane descent made his ears hurt. I was very proud of him, and they loved him.

The perfect baby bonding time was interrupted when Jeff was seven months old. Encouraged to join some friends for a few hours away at the nearby King's Hill ski area, we borrowed ski clothes and equipment and left Jeff with good friends, the Parks. Skiing was so much fun that a few weeks later, we went again. This unfortunate trip would separate me from Jeffrey for several days. I broke my right leg, the break spiraling from my right ankle up my tibia. In the base hospital, my heart felt shocked and bewildered. Half of me belonging to Don and baby Jeff was held up in a hospital bed in pain, unable to move. Poor Don was scrambling to care for two of us and work. Home from the hospital, I would be either in bed or wobbling on crutches into the nearby bathroom. Mother came for two weeks, and Elaine, a great air force wife from Alabama helped us for several hours each day after that. Jeff played on the bed with me as he could or as I could tolerate. Finally, on my feet again but still cast and on crutches, I tried to make up time with Jeff who was now scooting and later would walk before I did.

With Don's two years of active duty behind us, valuable grand-parent time was just ahead, and so were several adjusting moves. First up was our departure from Malmstrom Air Force Base, Jeff's birthplace, to Springfield, Missouri, when he was fifteen months old. We settled into the two extra bedrooms at my parent's house, the Davolts. Grandparents add such delightful approving love and get to burst into the law of scheduling and routines created by parents. It meant a parenting break now and then for us too. This was our first. It was good. But the next move to El Dorado Springs, new church, and two houses later happened all before baby #2 was announced. New friend Judy Gerster fell in love with Jeff and loved him through those changes. The first finger of Jeff's right hand had a nice cal-lous caused by sucking until he was promised a standing punching bag and Superman suit if he stopped. No problem. He did it. Mrs. Wright, our neighbor, helped too by bringing him daily treats.

When baby brother Jason was born, Jeff stood without a word against the wall just watching this nursing Christmas baby. This was what I had feared. My heart broke as I remembered the term "sibling rivalry" from books read. I drew fearful conclusions in my mind. Things improved greatly when Daddy bonding time began, as if on schedule.

Jeffrey had dark brown thick hair, huge beautiful eyes, long del-icate fingers, and all the natural growing spurts with giggling tickles in between. He took his time speaking and trying sounds. No worries to those who do.

The scariest events came with asthmatic spells he had following illness, fever, or viruses. One night, Don had to rush him to the hospital for a shot so he could breath. My heart beat wildly as I paced the hall while they were gone.

Just to jump on his red motorcycle with training wheels, get off and shoot some baskets, roll in the grass with Phillip, pick up a bat for T ball, or bounce the basketball again made for a busy energetic happy day and needed nap time. There was soccer, swimming, football, BMX biking, and skateboarding. Yet these flyby years found both Jeff—eighteen—and me dumbfounded in his bedroom looking at the prospect of moving him to college. Everything had suddenly fast-forwarded on us as Meadow Gold B.B. became Jr. High B.B. became High School B.B. became a B.B. scholarship to Northwest College in Kirkland Washington and became a degree at George Fox College playing basketball on another B.B. scholarship.

For now, Jeff's six-foot-five frame lay on his bed full length as I hustled around him moving a few college bound items here and there. "Will you need a trash can?" I asked stupidly. We both proceeded to laugh ourselves into tears when Jeff responded in his clueless way, and we both realized that neither of us had been down this road before, him going to college or me, releasing him.

"I don't know what I need," he said while I was still hearing the boy in him say, "Ask Dad to come pray with me!" This was his request on any night, if Don was not home yet and when the boys were settled in bed. Praying together was always the final sacred step to the end of each day.

My tears flowed now as they did with every mile from Seattle to Spokane on the return trip when we took him to the coast for college. The trip itself in our loaded red 1978 suburban was not without events either. In a way, the breakdown lightened the mood. Tami Holtz rode with us, and we each came to attention when the unusual slipping, grinding sound in the suburban shook us. The drive chain began to slip on the suburban while driving the passes in Idaho. We coasted silently into a little town that had no service, and prayerfully, we rolled on to Wallace. Dave Smith maintenance shop in Kellogg, Idaho, came to the rescue. We had to leave the suburban, rent a vehicle, unload, and reload it to get the first year of college started.

The campus was gorgeous and friendly. Eighteen years at home seemed suddenly a blink of an eye as we entrusted Jeff to higher learning and our Higher Father. His two years there were fun to hear about. We met his friends, the fellas, and counseled on the unexpected accidents from afar, the games (some of which we saw), the classes—all were a mixture of delight and long-distance agony.

What a loving gentle giant Jeffrey Alt Spurgeon is this day. He could pick at, exacerbate Jason, and produce fights out of thin air, sending one or both boys skipping steps to see who could exclaim the fastest and loudest, "*Mom!* He—!"

In spite of that, Jeff disciplined his choices toward good at a very early age, saying, "That's nasty," as he turned the TV off or changed the channel. Jesus became his own Savior during our time at Westside Baptist Church when he spoke with Pastor Eddie Neese. We prayed for him as he prayed for his friends, desiring that they know Jesus and salvation. He made a list of unsaved friends and has seen many of those prayers answered. Rick Shrum and Kurt Meske were on that list. He received the baptism of the Holy Spirit at the memorable C-N Family Camp when Dan Wagenman prayed for him. He would later take his own family to worship at church every Sunday and enjoy playing with his boys as much as they did with him.

Now a successful and personable business owner, his starting 7.50 an hour wage out of college has grown to provide for a family of five. Long and early hours, many phone calls to clients—who affirm the quality and caring personality of Jeff as one of the finest men they have ever known—follow his reputation. He is our frequent caller and "let's get together" planner.

I hardly take credit although I was home, cooking, cleaning, directing traffic, listening, and passing on the importance of a God-led and focused life. Many mistakes covered by God's grace, I stand grateful for the miracle of birth and the supreme blessing of a tender, sensitive if monstrous son, Jeffrey Alt Spurgeon released to His care.

# Chapter 20

## THE LITTLE GRAY BOX

*J*une of 1989, we celebrated twenty-five years of marriage. Thankful to finally be at 35 Green Ridge Lane, we did not want to spend very much money. We had been celebrating a new, never expected chapter of our lives, so we decided on a dinner at home. Jason suited himself in a white shirt with red bow tie and red suspenders to be our catered dinner server. We had three couples and our pastor who joined us and prayed over us as well. Several months later, the twenty-fifth anniversary was realized in a different sort of way.

\* \* \*

My heart skipped a beat, and I anxiously looked around with a questioning look on my face. "Oh well, it couldn't be lost." I decided. "Things always show up," I said to myself. "This will too. I'll just check pockets and retrace my steps as I have time."

"Hi, honey, the man came to look at the trailer," I called, non-chalantly being careful not to show concern when Don came home from work. "Supper will be ready when you get back inside," I yelled.

*I will not tell my husband about my missing ring*, I planned. *There is no reason to alarm him. We have a lot going on and are leaving for four days next week*, I rumbled in my mind. *I will begin to backtrack my steps, and it will show*, I thought with faith as I prayed the same.

*It would be awful, if lost for good, but I will watch the floor and carpet for any glimmers or sparkles.* I remembered Belle, a friend of mine, who had lost her diamond out of her setting once and a long time afterward, she "caught" sight of a sparkle across the room near a chair's edge and in the carpet. It was her diamond! "Oh well, it will be found," I confided to myself.

*It can't be lost*, I continued. I remembered that on our twenty-fifth wedding anniversary, we had jointly decided that being in our newly built house for almost a full year and having absorbed all the unexpected expenses was quite enough to celebrate, and no gifts were expected for this special anniversary. But that was when the little gray box showed up on June 13, and as I shook it, I prophet-ically said, "What is this, a rock?" recalling our no-gift agreement. It was a rock all right! My knees were weak, and my mouth gapped open when I peered into the gray jewelry container housed inside the gray ribboned box. When I shook it, the box in a box had felt and sounded just like a rock, perhaps as a joke, I had thought for a moment.

No, it was a *real* three-quarter carat single diamond dancing in the reflected kitchen light. It was on a thin gold band. I could wear it with my wider gold wedding band that Don had made me while in dental school.

"Chuck told me about this woman in Great Falls who deals with gems," Don said as he journeyed through the purchase story. I was only half-listening. "It has a slight flaw," he told me as he held it up to the light.

"I can't see a flaw!" I said as I gratefully slipped it on my finger for the first look.

That was almost a year ago. And now, so soon, I was contemplating the loss of so special a moment and gift. No tears came, just more determination and resolve that *I will check all purses and oh yes, the van and all my jackets, turn on the lights, and watch for anything shiny . . . before I tell Don,* I decided.

Nothing. And again, nothing. By now, the loss and sentimentality had struck my heart somewhere in the center of my chest with a feeling of heaviness. I was needing to tell someone. I had no choice but to confess the loss. I knew I was a bit too casual about some things such as keys, and checking to lock doors or covering items in the car to discourage would-be thieves.

"Did you check the washing machine or the camper?" Don offered when I told him. "We can place an ad in the paper, saying, 'Solitaire Diamond Ring Lost.'"

"What about a reward, and how much is it worth to you?" my husband quizzed. It seemed a lot, but we agreed on 500.00.

"But the ad will just come out, and we have to be gone for four days," I hopelessly offered.

We put the ad in anyway, and while gone, we wondered. It was days after our return when the phone rang. "Would you describe your diamond?" I heard the woman's voice say.

My heart began to beat faster as I swallowed and stuttered. "The band is bent on one side, and you can see a little line where the size was adjusted, and the diamond has a slight flaw not noticeable to the eye. And one prong looks more silverish than the other," I rattled.

"No, this is definitely not your ring," came the convincing voice.

I literally shouted as I heard myself say out loud, "Oh, please, Lord, let this be my ring!" I told her about the last time I remembered having it. "I could have taken it off at the college swimming pool or gone to the post office. I later filled up my van at the Conoco station on 10th. You know, the Kum and Go one!" I chattered on and finally rested my case. There was a hopelessly long pause.

"Without a doubt," she said, "this *is* your ring. I had it checked out already and was going to have a necklace made of it. I found it just outside my car at the Conoco gas station and later saw your ad of a week ago." I couldn't believe the change in her! I was happy beyond words, to say the least.

"Go to the bank and get five one-hundred dollar bills to have in case it is your ring," Don instructed after I got off the phone.

The caller and I agreed to meet at Gallery 16, my work day. My breath caught in my throat in anticipation when she walked in the door. The thrill to see the lost found dispelled the heaviness of loss. The ring looked small to me since I had enlarged it during the loss. It also seemed bittersweet to hand the money over, but the thrill of claiming ownership again still causes my eyes to join the sparkle of the once-lost ring, now found.

# *Chapter 21*

## JASON GRANT: BREAKING THROUGH

egardless of the time of year, Portland, Oregon, seemed to have flowers or trees that are budding and growing, and displaying their beauty. Our time visiting Jeff, Tricia, Jake, Joshua, and Justin was ending. We had reconnected, watched the boys play football, and gone to church with them. We planned to leave early morning of the next day to avoid the usual rush hour traffic. Our fifth wheel RV was ready to roll as we crawled into bed around 9:30 p.m. September 9, 2009.

Suddenly, our half-asleep mid-slumber was interrupted as Don's cell phone gave us that waking up sudden jolt.

It was Sam, Jason's friend, the tow-head blonde toddler who was two years old when the boys first met. Seldom if ever had he called us, but his voice was easy to recognize. He often referred to our son as Jaybird. Jason and Sam were living together with two other fellow friends near San Diego.

"Don't worry," he said, "we've just had a little 'hic up' today. Jason is all right. I'm here with him at the hospital. He wanted me to call you. There was a helicopter accident today."

Jason, who watched the skies for airplanes at an early age and had surprised us by saying the four syllable word *hel-o-cop-ter*, about the time he also said, "Mo-to-cy-le," was a licensed pilot now and had worked in several large cities flying for news agencies reporting current news. He also had flown tours at the Grand Canyon. We flew capriciously with him when he had 50 hours of flying time and later in the Grand Canyon when he had over 1900 hours. We respected his sensitivity to the "bird" and his careful expertise.

But now, questions and concerns of all kinds ran rampantly through our minds. *How seriously injured is he? Does he need us? What happened? Should we go to California instead of home to Montana?"* Jason assured us by phone that he not only had experienced a miracle in the last few hours, but also that we did not need to come. We wrestled the decision through the night. Knowing we could fly down if needed, we drove soberly and prayerfully back to Montana reflecting on Jason's life, these new concerns, and especially his injuries.

We had prayed for this son Jason Grant, at least six months before his conception. I knew almost immediately the signs of this pregnancy before medically confirmed. I felt so sick and could feel flutters and movement so early that I prayed that this tiny person was all right. I confessed my fears to a Christian friend Betty, who had given birth to five children, and I was consoled that all was well.

Jason's birth on December 22, 1969, was the best of all presents. The night of his birth, Don sang in a Christmas choir. I held two-and-a-half-year-old Jeffrey on my shortened knees made so by the big 9lb 14 3/4 ounce boy who would arrive just about six hours later and after our hurried forty-five minute drive to Nevada, Missouri. I can still hear the night nurse when she came in with Jason. "Feed this baby!" she said. It seems he was most unhappy with the bottle service there and was choosing me instead. The music from the previous evening about Mary giving birth lingered in my head, and I was definitely in tune with the wonder of that holy Christmas night when Christ was born. I felt enormously in tune with that world-changing moment.

The medicine with codeine given me caused hallucinations, and I was a miserable mess in that old hospital. Seeing Jason and his fat soft cheeks was my best medicine. I loved him at first sight, and we proudly brought him home on Christmas day in a small infant carrier appearing dwarfed by his size. Life definitely changed for our family. Jason ate often, smiled early, and was wide awake at 10:00 p.m. when we relished sleep.

This gift, our son Jason Grant, with a middle name from my father's first name, Grand, could find attention in strange places. Once, when he was a chubby six-month-old, his bare bottom embraced the baby bed rails while lying on his tummy with legs dangling down in a hilarious position. In seconds, his fingers could reach the open Vaseline jar beside his bed or stand on tiptoes for the extra inch to reach whatever. The Christmas gum drop tree that I made for decoration on his first birthday was considered his "own" personal treat as he helped himself. On occasion, his cuisine included dog food and sand.

Marla, our fourteen-year-old neighbor's daughter adored him. The neighbors in El Dorado Springs and church family all rejoiced at his birth. Anna, an older neighbor on our street, shared his birth date and on the twenty-second of December, his first birthday, made him a cake. It was on that proud day he began to take his first steps. Before school age, a television program called the *Friendly Giant* grabbed his attention. The giant played a musical recorder, and of course, Jason did too while he sat on a little bench wearing his hat engrossed in giant pursuits and later reenacted the giants pursuits with his G.I. Joe guys, which he strung down stairways using string, duct, or masking tape. We remembered that as he grew, his grade school teachers loved him too and wrote on his end-of-school comments a wish that he would always keep his happy smile. This individualistic and creative boy dressed for school as he wanted, even against the norm on occasion. Shoes were the best, like the new white with red and blue tennis shoes or first cowboy boots snuggled in his arms against him at bedtime as he went off to sleep.

As we traveled, we remembered together how his life had been spared another time in a near fatal accident involving a church van with thirteen high school students. The van they were riding in overshot an exit outside of Great Falls, sending bodies flying out as it rolled several times. These beautiful kids ended up in the hospital emergency room with various injuries. The group was going to attend high school days at Northwest College where Jeff was attending. At impact, Jason was lifted out of his shoes as his head hit the top of the sliding side door, and the momentum tossed him into a field. He received a huge open-handed-sized concussion on the top of his head along with shoulder, knee, and eye injuries. At the time the phone call came to me at home, Jason was already arriving by ambulance at the emergency room. I left immediately to drive across town. We had no cell phones then, and no one answered at Don's office. *How could I reach Don?* God miraculously had us meet at an intersection near the hospital at the exact same time. We recognized each other. I waved frantically, and Don turned around and followed. Jason was a tenth grader then. His life was saved; however, his injuries left a significant follow-up trail adding to two prior events, a leg and clavicle break.

As we traveled toward home and not San Diego, there were some reassurances with these memories. Being a curious and "traveling" eight–month-old, while living in El Dorado Springs, I watched Jason with horror as he maneuvered his heavy four-wheeled Cadillac (an older fashioned wood and metal stroller walker combination) beyond my running grasp toward some stairs. When the clunky transportation bounced over the steps and hit the landing, his little body flew out hitting his head against a wall. His head was turned to the right. I gathered him up and immediately took him to Dr. McGee to be checked. Many years later, his neck vertebrae showed an irregularity during a sports physical, and the doctor questioned the safety factor of him playing football. It was a difficult decision to make. I struggled with it, but he played anyway, from sixth grade and into his senior year. An unfortunate second clavicle break sadly ended his football aspirations early in his senior season.

"Should we go now to San Diego?" we continued. Jason reported to us from his hospital room that they hoped to avoid surgery by fitting him with a full brace for the thoracic, lumbar, and cervical compressions he suffered in the accident. His phone numbers were lost in the crash, and his cell phone was never recovered.

I made calls for him from Montana as he directed while we awaited doctor's reports. Helplessly lying in a hospital in Escondido, California, near the crash site was in sharp contrast to the successful athlete of baseball, soccer, basketball, biking, skateboarding, track, downhill skiing, football, and volleyball guy we knew. Here lay the homecoming king and the spiritual leader in his youth group who was reading his Bible from an early age and chosen to sing and perform with the esteemed Chanteur Choir. He had worked as a mechanic, a grocery bag clerk, a Glacier Park summer employee, a waiter at Bert'n Ernie's restaurant, and later at Community Hospital in Missoula, first as a volunteer orderly, then in physical rehabilitation, and later after his degree, as a diagnostic testing specialist for psychiatry in the hospital and again for a forensic psychologist.

His degrees in biology and psychology accomplished, he thought seriously about becoming a physician assistant. He helped Don in his dental office some while in high school, and his understanding of science and math made a medical profession a consideration. However, with increasing competition for entrance, he was not accepted. It was a disappointment after a very successful interview in California.

Always able to get a job, his creative bent and analytical nature kept him searching unable to settle for the right path until his love and early interest in flying won out. "Top Gun" won! Not exactly. After and with many hours of flying and successful testing, he was at last a licensed and, a short time later, a credentialed instructor.

Now with this accident, weeks passed as the Federal Aviation Administration (FAA) began the investigation of the single helicopter crash. Was it pilot error or mechanical? The helicopter had literally fallen from the sky from less than seventy-five feet while coming in to a practice field landing. He and his passenger pushed through the clouds of debris, pushed open the doors to crawl away from the explosion that might happen next. Thankfully, there was no fire. The rotor blades were ripped away, and the skids splintered out in a squat, but the cab had remained upright, even on a rocky hillside due largely to God's protection and Jason's last-minute emergency skills he executed, which now he re-ran over and over in his mind.

When the FAA finally had their report, we joined Jason in breathing a healthy sigh of relief with much thanksgiving. At this point, Jason was still reliving and analyzing every second before the crash. The cam shaft was proven faulty, cracked in two on the fallen new helicopter, a manufacturing defect. He and his passenger suffered the same back compression injuries. They compared notes sympathetically for a while and then disputed an insurance release form and parted ways.

We did not go to San Diego. We recounted the tragedy-turned-miracle every day. As Don would say, "He can move his fingers and toes and walk." Jason's last job denied insurance coverage. That was a real blow. With no income, his recovery care was minus the immediately needed rehabilitation and therapy. His back and related muscles were in constant pain. A number level of comfort one to ten wasn't possible to judge because being upright for five to ten minutes were consistently intolerable for him for many months. Sensitive to God, we knew that Jason's Bible was near him, even at this difficult time.

Progress and healing were slow. He somehow traveled to his namesake grandfather's funeral in Missouri in October and back to California while in his body cast. The long year and a half wait involving lawyers and insurance and the manufacturer of the faulty helicopter began. Unable to work, symptoms of posttraumatic distress syndrome targeted him mentally. The ocean and surfing became a refuge and still is.

> Where do I go from your Spirit?
> Where can I flee from Your presence?
> If I go up to the heavens, You are there;
> If I make my bed in the depths,
> You are there-You are there.
> If I rise on the wings of the dawn,
> If I settle on the far side of the sea,
> Even there Your hand will guide me,
> Your right hand will hold me fast.
> You and there. You are there.

If I say, "Surely the darkness will hide me
And the light become night around me,
Even the darkness will not be dark to You
The night will shine like the day
*For darkness is as light to You."*
Psalm 139:7–12 (NIV)

Many miles keep separating us, yet this man—our son—found a way to be near us to visit his aging grandfather for many special bonding times as well as giving us support before his death; the same son-man came when Don and I had surgeries to check on us and lend support. The same man became our handsome waiter for our silver wedding anniversary spreading Reynolds's wrap down all the halls and paths in the house as a surprise. He had time for elk hunts with his dad when possible and still sits on the kitchen counter to talk to me when at home for a visit.

As a parent, turning back the time to blessed memories of safety, love, and laughter, teasing and growing, praying and more love brings focus to the present—the dreams and building from little invites the divine. He has it in His hand, much like the keys to the black Nissan pickup, adorned with a brilliant and very large red bow. Those keys are still around. Like his father tells others as he shares the lavish love of our saving Christ. Here is the package with all you need, but you have to take it to receive what is in it, opening the windows of heaven so that we cannot even contain it as Malachi 3:10 promises.

To my son: "Please watch where you are running, take it easy on your head. No poles to run into requiring stitches, okay? Run instead into another monster elk like Hugo or, better yet, the arms of love—Jesus and me."

Did I mention surfing? hockey of late? Housebuilding? *And flying once more?*

# Chapter 22

## NO FEAR IN LOVE

We liked her right away and soon learned that her life had made a responsible and settling turn. She loved her new profession of dental assisting, and she was good. She moved and talked like an efficient waitress.

She came to Montana from the South and had lived here and there. She was raised largely by her grandmother, worked in bars, and lived with Phil. The route of her life had taken many turns not all the best, but as her time in the office lengthened, a new steadiness seemed to develop. Blonde, happy, smiley, bright eyes, and about five feet two or three, her name was Kathy Buchanan, a student at the vocational technical school, ambitious and assigned to Don's dental office for her practical hours as a dental assistant.

She was good with patients and very efficient. She appreciated everything. Don offered her a job at the office after her practicum, and the professional pride she demonstrated benefited everyone. She finally got her own apartment, and on several occasions, I remember picking her up there so she could visit Calvary Community Church with us.

Jeff, our seventeen-year-old son, worked for Don in the office a couple of summers. He and Kathy hit it off well. She became a good office buddy for him.

It was a Monday in May. "I wonder why she isn't here this morning?" everyone was asking. LaVada, the office receptionist, was not in until noon, so the work schedule had to be adjusted because of Kathy's absence. Finally, the phone rang. It was Kathy's voice. "I will be a little late, maybe there by twelve o'clock," she said. "I got a late start from Bozeman this morning. I was at my brother's for the weekend," she said apologetically. This did not seem like Kathy who could always be counted on to be prompt and on time.

Noon came, and as usual, the staff departed for lunch. And since the office was near the hospital, it was common to hear the beater sound or see the red and white Mercy Flight helicopter coming in for a landing. Jeff remembered looking up and seeing the beautiful clear blue sky with colorful helicopter in view.

Another call came. Kathy had been in an accident near Great Falls. She had almost made it home.

Everyone and everything in the office seemed to be on pause. Kathy was alive but in intensive care. Patients were cancelled, calls made, visits began. I was called to come into town to meet Don at the hospital.

"Can you hear us, honey?" Phil, her boyfriend, was saying to the swollen beyond-recognition bruised face. Her hands were swollen too. Her head was bandaged, and her eyes were closed. Bruising was anywhere we could see skin.

Helpless, we waited and prayed for this beautiful and vivacious girl to wake up or move, even a little finger.

A brother was coming, and other relatives were notified of the seriousness of the accident. Her grandmother from Livingston, whom we had not met before, came also. She spoke of Kathy as her "Rose," which was her middle name.

Don happened to know the officer who was first on the scene of the accident. Kathy hit a guard rail on the interstate near Cascade, Montana, and was catapulted from the small car she was driving. Her body hit a telephone pole and came to rest in a sitting position at its base. She was not conscious when he found her.

We were told right away that the swelling of her brain from the extreme trauma made her chances of survival questionable.

"Why?" we said as our tears mingled with those of others waiting. "Did she fall asleep while driving?" we wondered. "What was the real story in Bozeman? Would we know?"

Our disbelief and shock were mixed in with the time, season, her youth, and life coming together that we had observed so happily. Minutes ticked into the next day but barely. Kathy died just after midnight on May 19, 1987.

Kathy left us all too tragically.

Don and I sang "Thank God for the Promise of Springtime" at the funeral. It seemed to be our prayer offering and faith declaration. Bert Murphy prayed and conducted the small service at the Chapel of Chimes.

After the service, the strangest thing happened. A woman we knew well pulled me aside to secretly tell me about a rumor. "Don't be surprised," she said. Someone had said that Dr. Spurgeon was having an affair with Kathy.

"What?" I gasped, but that statement was so ludicrous we immediately dropped it from any consideration. Even gossip ramifications flounder without nourishment. End of story.

Char, who was a hygienist at the office, handstitched a beautiful cross-stitched memorial plaque, which we framed with Kathy's happy face placed at the top. That touching memorial lived on at the office wall until Don's retirement.

We both loved Kathy. We still love her. Our Jeff remembers and loves her. "There is no fear in love," just the unforgettable loss and brief moment of a life we embraced and miss.

# Chapter 23

## NEW LIFE, REALLY?

"Do you want to be called Nana or Grandma?" they asked. Was Don going to be a granddad, a grandpa, or a papa? *What is life without new birth?* We chose Nana and Papa. It was great to get to choose, but we really didn't care. We were still getting used to the idea and wondering what it meant to be one of each. We still wonder at times as my parents and Don's family must have wondered when our U-Haul en route to Montana departed to live so far from them. We just know for certain the blessing of grandchildren is amazing.

Jacob Alt Spurgeon was born on November 27, 1996 in Portland, Oregon. He was expected that day, but I had no idea I would feel so special miles away. I went to work at the gallery that day but remember the delight in my heart, unlike any feeling I had experienced before. Somehow, my chest enlarged with gratitude or pride, and my breathing quickened. As I got out of the car at Gallery 16 and opened the door from the alley, all of life had changed as this little namesake to the Spurgeon family's name ran through my mind. He now had become the fourth generation to have the middle name of Alt, the name of a medical school professor of Dr. Marion Eaton Spurgeon, country doctor and Jacob's great-great-grandfather. So we now had Adrian Alt, Jacob Alt's great grandfather; Don Alt, Jacob's grandfather; and Jeffrey Alt, Jacob's dad. Imagine that! We were honored and surprised perhaps because the possible names were not shared ahead of time, and the sex of the awaited was unknown. About two weeks after Jacob's birth, I went to Portland by invitation. Skye puppy, the first "child," was Jacob's protector and stood tall on the bed above the bassinet protecting the almost 8 lbs new master.

Nana babysat one evening while the new mommy and daddy went to a Christmas party. I rocked him and talked to him. I prayed with him, and we listened to a ballgame on the little radio near his crib. He was a fine fella with enormous eyes like his daddy Jeff.

Jacob boy,

you were such a sleepy head before you "came alive," then you
saw the Christmas lights. "Did you give your Daddy five?"
Skye puppy ate an ornament, and the tree almost fell,
three diapers in one changing, but Daddy's voice you could tell!
In only two weeks, eight and a half pounds, one inch. "Fol-
low through and jump shots, not you on the bench."
First night in the big bed, Blazers game was on.
Gramma Nana read Genesis and the Christmas story long.
Mama up in the night, burps, diapers, and sleep,
Skye watching you closely, safeguarding to keep.
And Nana, what fun to see you laugh;
You're so smart, so cute, and she gave you a bath!
'Round the kitchen you went like a football in hand,
"Stop that, father, I know you have plans!"
In your mama's eyes, room, music, and toys
I see God's blessing on this Jacob boy.

# Chapter 24

## CRAZY WIND

The light from the bathroom filtered softly into the early dark morning over the oyster-colored carpet onto our bed and blankets as the wind, like a tunneled shaft of sounding motion, pushed the remaining dried stalks of rose bush stems against the bay window. Don was getting out of the shower as usual at about 6:00 a.m. The house was dark except for those same lines of soft light. Another day was about to begin.

My sluggish mind, slow to wake up on any morning, heard the wind. The wind was, however, the norm for where we live. I was half awake and half asleep. My eyes opened with a start, and I was on my feet in an instant when the sudden pounding and slamming on the same bay window started. Yelling at Don as I moved toward the window, I wondered at the wisdom of opening the large shade really not knowing what would be on the other side of the window. The pounding was urgent. We pulled the blind up.

The roaring wind muffled with the shouts of Sherri, our neighbor, as we saw with horror and disbelief her silhouette against the orange-lit sky, its light now spreading into our bedroom. Her mouth was open wide with the movement of the unheard shouts, and her eyes showed fear. The middle large window of the bay window three-some showed leaping yellows, oranges, reds, and white sparks on the edges like an artist's canvas as a backdrop to her silhouette. The scene behind her now is sealed in my memory.

The McKinleys, whose house was built about the same time as ours in 1989, lived just to the North and West of us and across a graveled road. Don and I ran from the bedroom to the front door to meet her, and as we opened the door against the high winds, we were knocked back with the force, left gapping at Sherri as she ran on to alert more unsuspecting neighbors. I grabbed a robe as we ran to the garage. Don did not say anything. He found nearby shovels as he ran. Both of us headed down the driveway toward the gravel road that separated us from the flaming inferno that was crowding the dark sky. If the flames licked across the road, the grasses and wind would carry the fire dangerously toward three homes, including ours. The sparks were landing in our field on our side of the road. As Don ran, his pace quickly left me behind, and I stopped midway down the driveway, asking myself defenselessly, "What do I do next?"

I walked backward with a huge feeling of insignificance, and the following thought came to me as I simultaneously turned my back on the fire, lifted my hands into the air to pray. In prayer, I said, "It's all Yours. It's all Yours," over and over. It was a type of releasing prayer that brought peace. The high winds and bellowing flames made the situation seem impossible even though I looked back to see two smaller fire trucks nearing the McKinley house.

The roar of the flames and wind in my ears were strangely shut out when I got back inside the house, which was unbelievably calm and quiet. I grabbed the phone and began dialing any memorized numbers with a quick plea to ask for prayer against the wind and flames.

The consuming fire in the grassy field now blocked the view of the McKinley's house across the road, meaning the fire could leap onto their roof any time. Faint touches of daylight were trying to enter the orange and black scene to the East as the smoke began rising from the water now used for protection near their house.

By now, I had my car keys in hand.

Suddenly, as if by command, the wind took a breath. The whipping sound deafened. The sparks fell, and the roar lowered by decimals. The change was startling. I blinked to test the reality of the moment. At the same time, I heard myself uttering the voluntary expressions: "Thank You, Lord. Thank you, Lord. Thank you, Lord!"

The fire and wind died a few feet from the McKinley's house and did not cross the graveled road.

"Even the wind and waves obey him" (Matt. 8:27), "Peace Be Still (Mark 4:7).

# Chapter 25

## A VIEW IN THE STREET

"I think I will drive Jason's Ford Bronco today," Don said. "It has that For Sale sign in it. Maybe it will interest a passerby, employee, or somebody!" Jason tore the insides out of this vehicle completely and replaced parts, sanded, repainted it, and spent many hours lying on his back or crawling around and under it to get it looking and running well.

It was a 1984 boxy type style and was his transportation for about three years while he was in Missoula working at Community Hospital.

It was Thursday. I work on Thursdays at Gallery 16. On March 2, 1998, and after his work at the office on Thursdays, Don went to exercise with a class at the Health Works Fitness Studio in the 1200 hundred block of Central Avenue downtown. Since his office was east and south in Gt. Falls, he often traveled 25th street to Central where he turned left and drove toward downtown.

And so, on this particular evening about 5:30 p.m., it was still daylight when I left the gallery to go home. I pulled away from the alley behind Gallery 16 at 608 Central and, as usual, headed home going East on Central Avenue.

About a block or so before Paris Gibson Square Museum of Art at 15th Street, I realized the cars were backed up, and I briefly considered choosing another route. However, it was at the same moment I saw a tall man in the middle of the street ahead removing his coat. The coat looked airborne as it swung up then down and to the pavement.

I was shocked. His image, his coat, his height became my husband, Don. And at the same moment, I saw another image being covered by his coat lying on the pavement. There were people starting to gather as I pulled quickly up over the curb to the right, jumped out running with a multitude of questions echoing in my mind. *That's Don! That's Don! That's Don!* I repeated in disbelief.

I must have flown across the street. It seemed I was instantly at his side taking in as much as I could of the tragic scene. He was feeling the pulse of this young woman with dark hair who looked to be thirty or forty. Other people were saying, "I saw it happen" or "I can be a witness" as the flashing lights and officers arrived. "She ran right into you against the light," a witness said.

"How fast were you traveling?" asked the officer while other officers were measuring and marking the street and taking photos.

I laid my hand on his shoulder, but absorbed with the girl, he seemed not to know I was there. Don stayed in his position knelt over the girl, never leaving her until the ambulance arrived, and together, we released her to the emergency crew.

The air was somewhat suffocating. There were papers to sign, more questions and responses from witnesses, and numbers to exchange. In days ahead, we both would recall many statements and fill in what we remembered.

As he was driving, Don remembered crying aloud, "No! Don't do that!" when he pushed hard on the brakes at the moment he saw her and the instant of impact, which sent the body into the air, landing several feet away.

Recounting moments prior and after, we remembered that the sun was shining, the cars were two or three deep, all stopped at the

15th Street stoplight, waiting for the light to turn green on Central. As the traffic and Don started to move, the woman ran across two lanes of moving traffic on Don's left and out of his sight to strike Jason's left headlight and grill in the third lane over.

I hugged Don who stood in shock, saying, "I'll see you at the hospital."

Our church was on Central Avenue and on my route to the hospital. I suddenly found myself pulling up the alley and into the parking lot and running to the back door. I ran into the building, hoping to see anyone for strength, comfort, or, more importantly, prayer.

There was a weight loss group of eight to ten people meeting in the North Fireside room. I ran to them, interrupting them with, "Don just hit a woman on Central Avenue!" The next thing I remember seems unusual now, but all jumped to their feet as a common reaction with the immediacy they felt for the situation. They began to pray spontaneously for her safety and us too. This gave me great comfort when others joined us in prayer. The timing was of God.

I don't know who called our pastor and wife, or friends, LaVada, and Bert Murphy, but soon, the waiting room was filled with prayer and Lindy's mother. I kept watching her trying to imagine how I would feel toward us, unknown people placed in her life so suddenly, with the life of her daughter now at risk. We stayed until 10:30 p.m. and learned that Lindy—a single mom with three children—was a runner who, recovering only two weeks from an abdominal hysterectomy, had decided to go for a run, against her doctor's orders. Her mother confessed her daughter's troubled past, which did not ease the guilt or gravity of what we felt had happened just a few hours before.

Our prayers continued. We visited Lindy in the hospital, sent cards, flowers, and called her parents often. She was out of intensive care on March 5. She complained most about a headache. Miraculously, no bones were broken. When I visited her, I remember getting a cold towel for her head, and she was appreciative and kind to me in this totally dark room. She went home in about a week.

The day after the accident, the front page of the *Tribune* announced, "Dr. Hits Jogger on Central," with a small incident explanation. That did not feel good. However, we began to receive calls and notes of concern and understanding. And concerned we were. I took food to the apartment where Lindy's mother was tending to her toddler who was about two years old and one older son. A third teenage son lived in Helena. Lindy had recently moved from Havre to Great Falls.

Several weeks later, the story became even more tragic. Lindy was found deceased on her living room sofa by her mother. Our concerns grew. As always, the choice exists to run to our merciful God or to run away. We ran to Him.

We attended the funeral. We felt out of place among those attending. Afterward, we left town in the pickup and drove toward Canada for a mental rest and change. We went to the Lethbridge Hotel and did nothing. There was a balcony that opened to the middle where a swimming pool was in view. We stood, watched, and talked. We both recalled that on the way home, a big rock hit the windshield. The results still show on the grey 96 Dodge's windshield. We seemed in a stream traveling against an uncertain tide of events. We expected a law suit and waited, keeping the statements and file of information. We even visited a lawyer for advice. Our grief for an unknown person, even if troubled, was real and confusing.

About three weeks after the funeral, we received an unexpected call. A pastor's wife we knew at the time was also the secretary at the funeral home office.

"Carol, the death certificate on Lindy came to us," she said. "It is not to be public property. Do not tell anyone I called you. It says that Lindy died of an alcohol/drug overdose."

We learned more about her difficult past later, but at the time, our friend's call was as if God himself had phoned us. We were somewhat relieved but still so sorry.

We had not heard anymore concerning this life tragedy until about a year ago, a gentleman at church said, "I need to talk to you!" My mind tried to think of anything he could need to tell us. It seemed rather urgent and with a note of excitement.

He began with, "My son pastors a church in Bozeman," he said. "There is a young man in his church who just recently asked Christ to come into his life. My son baptized him last Sunday. He was the youngest son of a Lindy Sutherland.

"A comforting word to hear, indeed. We are comforted. His name is Joseph."

# Chapter 26

## NEW LIFE WITH JOSHUA THOMAS

Thomas, with a middle name from his Branderhorst grandfather, was next to occupy the very special closet in the downstairs guest room. In fact, the bed happened to be the same baby bed that his own daddy and uncle Jason had used when they were born. It now had a new bumper pad, sheets, and the little pillow that Great-Grandmother Davolt had made while waiting for this big boy to come for his first stay. It would be our first time to hold him.

The day he was born, October 22, 1998, followed a time of loss in our families, so this new baby brought new life and promises just like Joshua in the Bible did. When we knew his name, we loved it, and we both hurried to the book of Joshua to see the character of this follower of God. We also had a new puppy bird dog that October. This puppy was pretty cute, but I just wanted to see and celebrate Joshua.

Because Joshua loved animals so much, maybe getting Mini at the same time was okay. Joshua was a very healthy boy and not afraid of us at all. Even Great-Grandpa Davolt got to see him on his first Christmas in Montana. Uncle Jason was turning thirty, Grandpa came to visit from Missouri, and Joshua was celebrated all at the same time. When Joshua first got up in the morning, he and Papa began a tradition of first sleepy snuggles and morning talks in the big blue chair.

# JOSHUA THOMAS SPURGEON

Early one morning
October twenty-two
Mama and Daddy
got all ready for you! Your room was warm
with sunlight bright Daddy, Jacob, and Oma
welcomed your sight!
You were big, all right
and handsome too. Beautiful hands:
bright eyes of blue.
What snuggles you gave,
little squeaky noise,
But no big cries
from your little voice.
Mama was happy with Jacob's new playmate, a Spurgeon
boy tradition and Opa, a namesake!
Joshua was strong,
believed the God he served.
Nana prays for courage
follow Jesus and discern all the purposes and future
only God designs
for happiness and love
special Joshua in mind.
Psalm 139
Love Nana, November 1998

# Chapter 27

## LEONARD

"Oh, Justina! Oh, my goodness! This is beautiful! Yes, I can use it! I can use it in many ways. I love it!" I exclaimed.

We had just arrived at Big Stone Colony, only a few miles from our house near Great Falls. My Hutterite friend scurried off and through a closed door and returned with my Christmas present. No, it wasn't Christmas. In fact, summer was near. We could tell that by the road side view of the gardens already planted, with rhubarb towering above the seedlings, some of which were safely covered with plastic.

"You didaaat come fo' Creeees-mus," she said with disappointment in her German accent. She reentered the small sitting room that housed the table, a chair, two benches and a small sewing table. I felt guilty. She was right. I was stammering in my mind, trying to think of why we did not make the traditional journey to the Colony in December.

More tragedy had entered the Entz family, and even that was several weeks ago. In her hands, Justina carried the large round glass relish plate, wrapped in a plastic grocery bag. The plate had six removable dishes placed around a center round bowl. And as she pointed out, the individual containers sat on another glass serving plate useful for a variety of foods. She was delighted with this sparkling glass and heavy gift given me. I wished to give it right back to her, seeing the pleasure she had in showing it.

Gift exchanging was a normal gesture in our friendship. I brought my small gift of cards and perfume. Don brought fresh donuts from IGA, and knowing that part of a memorial gift was recently used for bananas, we brought bananas too. Justina, a diabetic, said she would have a donut for lunch too.

My friend was busy emptying the table of gifts and even the fresh lilacs I had cut from our yard, when I stopped her and insisted on a hug. After all these years, I received a warm, softer lingering hug, a hug that spoke, "I am glad you are here, and I know you are sorry with me, and I accept your sympathy."

Our first visits to the colony began years ago when we went for fresh bread, eggs, or chickens. Justina was the head cook and soon insisted that when we came, we should come to her house, not the colony communal kitchen. So we began doing that and reacquainted ourselves each time with her and John's large family of ten children, her sisters, and many relatives. Through the years, we have taken many of our visiting guests there to meet and sample homemade root beer and wine, go to the kitchen, see the homemade steel vats for frying, the dining hall, and the chapel where they meet at 6:00 p.m. every day of the week for worship and readings by the head preacher. All the chapel benches glisten with varnish, competing with the clean shining vinyl flooring that not only covers the floor but also goes up the walls.

One time, we visited when they were butchering chickens, not just a few either. The men and women worked on this jointly, wore rubber knee-high boots on a water washed concrete floor, and had racks where chickens were placed in rows for various procedures of cleaning and washing, drying, and packaging. I believe they had processed six hundred that day. Another time we watched milking cows, attached to milking machines that drew the milk out into large waiting containers. The cows were on an elevated floor all heads facing center in a circular fashion. The process went on continuously, carefully tended by Hutterite men.

Only six weeks prior, the John Entz family had lost their third adult son. Our visit was bringing back memories of a call I received in the fall of 2009.

"There has been a tragedy here," Don said via cell phone to me. I was en route home, on highway 87 when he called, about ten minutes from home.

He continued, "I didn't want you to be shocked when you got here." He added, "I am okay."

As I came up the road, I saw the Mercy Flight helicopter first. Two deputy sheriff vehicles sat pointing downhill toward our white shed. Several people were standing around including several men dressed in the traditional black of the colony. I recognized Walter, one of the Entz boys, then a cousin Martin who came with Leonard to unload hay each fall from our flat bed trailer to the roofed area just behind the shed. They were just walking around in the yard. The job of lifting about one hundred plus bales of hay was a yearly job now anticipated by Leonard and Martin. It was extra money for them. Don gave them one hundred dollars to split. If Don didn't call them, they called him saying, "When do you get your hay?" These two boys in their twenties had to put up with Don's teasing about the girls or what they would spend the money on. They expected his teasing now, as they did the ice water and soda and the rides Don provided to and from the colony.

Leonard, a son of Justina's, was a tall thin fella, with blondish brown hair. He seemed to be the leader, and he and Martin were hardworking machines. They could unload a loaded flatbed trailer and truck within about an hour and a half.

On this particular evening, Leonard and Martin had moved about ten bales. Don had stepped out of sight to check on the drinking water and soda when Martin found him and reported that Leonard had sat down, saying he was dizzy. As Don raced following Martin, Leonard tumbled from the bale of hay he sat on to the ground and rolled several feet down the slope from where he had fallen.

Martin was circling now, while Don started the recommended steps of rescue cardiopulmonary resuscitation (CPR): holler for help, clear the airway, tilt head, blow into mouth, begin compressions all numbered and repeated rhythmically. Unbelief mixed with reality as each adrenaline surged second passed. A slight short response lapsed into the same breathless scene. Don had scrambled for one free hand to reach his cell phone, connected to 911, and continued the CPR as prescribed.

When I got out of the van, there was a hushed stillness hanging in the air. Walter, Dan, another brother, and Martin paced on the grass near the garage and out of sight of the immediate scene. I wanted to see Don but felt like an intruder at my own house entering a sacredly still and emotion-charged moment in our lives, yet we were apart. The hush had a death voice. What could I do? What question should I ask? Should I run to the shed? Was that appropriate?

All too soon we knew. Leonard was dead. This group of men and elders from the colony had just arrived. Justina, his mother, my friend, was not there. *Did she know?* I kept thinking. I wondered to myself who would tell her, "Your son who was alive this morning and at lunch, and at supper is now dead."

As is the custom, Hutterites do not use a mortuary but instead take their dead and prepare them for burial at the colony. In this case, they were required by law to take the body for an autopsy because of the situation of his death.

Story bits came to our hearing in time to help our understanding and ease some of the liability and questions we felt. Leonard had heart pills. Did he take them? What were they for? He had been resting midday of late. He told Martin before they started working, "I think I will be sick tonight." The hours that followed turned to a fog of reports to the sheriff and coroner, the departures of the helicopter and vehicles and Hutterite men. The colony preacher invited us to the impending wake. Walter had said words of comfort to me, sensing the deepening distress in me. Their departures settled into the reality. It was dark outside now and inside.

Don sat at the kitchen bar, thinking of Leonard's young age while I observed the raw skin on his hand near his thumb, rubbed blister-like by the continuous compressions he made on Leonard's chest until help arrived, about twenty minutes.

"Will they blame us?" I asked Don.

"Could I have done anything else to prevent his death?" Don followed.

Two days later, we attended the wake, usually for Hutterite colony members only. Leonard was wrapped in a thin-looking white material and laid in a handmade wooden coffin. His hands held something small and rather dainty for the rough and tough persona of a hard worker. With his large family sitting within inches all around him, the colony members—men on one side, women on the other—sang gustily back and forth. Interspersed with singing came the reading in German of single lines of rhetoric, none understood by us except the word *alleluia*.

We took flowers. Now three years later, Justina reminded us of what would have been Leonard's twenty-ninth birthday. Neither families drinks alcoholic beverages, but today, we drank—a swallow of cherry wine to these sons and our memories. It, as always, tastes horrible but turns strangely sweet.

The second son, Dan Entz, died as suddenly after Leonard, and now—only six weeks prior—the John Entz family lost a third son to the same heart irregularity. Sadly, we remembered not only Leonard but the tragic and just-as-sudden passing of Dan and now Walter who had walked the yard with me when Leonard died.

Walter's bride of a year and their one-year-old Daniel joined us now in the Entz sitting room, all sharing the little understood heart problem and triple loss.

Was Justina due a good soft and warm hug on this day when words were meaningless? I am thankful she reciprocated, and I will try harder not to disappoint her this next Christmas.

We left with soup in a jar and a package of store-bought cookies that John slipped into the car along with my glass serving dishes. Justina waved from the door and reminded me, calling out, "Save your empty jars for me, and come back sooner next time!"

# Chapter 28

## NEW LIFE FOR MY MAIN MAN

This time our response was, "Yes, another grandson!" We took the fifth-wheel trailer over to Beaverton to await his coming. We were to become the real Nana and Papa to Jacob, now five and a half, and Joshua, now three and a half when this new life was due. We would be there to look after these little boys. "We can *do* this!"

We will never forget taking them into a restaurant to eat, only to see barrels of peanuts everywhere for snacking. Some shells lay about on the floor. The boys had already found the game machines. We slowly began to panic inside and knew we had to get hands washed and out of there. As I recall it, we ended up having a tailgate supper in the back of the pickup while praying that Jacob, our ana-phylaxis-allergy-suffering grandson would not have a reaction to all those peanuts. We were to guard carefully these little boys while their momma and daddy awaited our visit to see Justin Michael Spurgeon for the very first time. I still feel like shaking. We are not alarmist, yet we both knew the danger we unknowingly placed Jacob in by being there. We began to settle down a bit when we saw this newest boy,

Justin Michael Spurgeon, packaged in a receiving blanket and little hat. We took our turns holding him while sensing this special God-given moment. Tricia was thinking about Jacob and Joshua and got into the floor with them and helped them work with a new specialty Lego project. I was amazed at her strength.

The next day, there were some concerns, and we prayed that Justin would respond with full function plumbing so he could come home. Our prayers were answered although his little crying squeaks indicated he was not getting nourished as he wanted. Momma began a steadfast journey to get him satisfied. Many miracles accompany this boy whose dimples and smile disarm and melt hearts. A corrected partial palatal cleft made eating easier, and various therapies have beneficially taught any motor skills that were lagging behind. We experienced big thrills, knowing all the activities he has accomplished in his young life from bike riding, basketball, running, and now swimming. The boys nick-named him the Duts, a term of endearment. Justin has the magical ability of bringing everyone together in a special loving way.

# I THINK HE'S A KEEPER

Dear Justin, this is Nana,
your grandmother in Montana
And your daddy's momma.
I got to see you when
you were only three hours old! That was a special joy in my life and made me very happy.
You also made your Daddy happy!
It made Nana happy to see how much you were
loved by your special Mommy
and Daddy!
Papa called you Squeaker because your
tiny cry sounded that way.
Your lungs will be strong because they got
extra exercise while everyone was learning your
language!
Nana and Papa are thankful for YOU!
We can't wait to see you grow big, laugh, talk, and walk,
but right now, we say a prayer of
thanksgiving for your life and all that God has in mind for you.
We agree with Him that you are wonderfully made
and
that His plans
for you are only for good!

# Author's Notes

God used a speaker at a senior's camp called West of 60s at Glacier Bible Camp, Montana, to inspire me. He spoke about legacy. I was encouraged to record my life in some way, especially highlighting the forever presence of Jesus Christ and His personal intervention and direction. I kept the speaker's notes near the computer in a stack for a couple of years as I contemplated what should be passed along. Timing was in my favor when a teacher of writing agreed to teach a workshop. Her book *Bound Like Grass* won the Best Book Award for that year in Montana. I read Ruth McLaughlin's book, a beautifully poetic memoir. I took the workshop and was invited to a small writing group that meets weekly. I haven't stopped writing, thanks to the Ghost Writers, my writing friends who have listened and kept me going toward a goal. My ambition goes only as far as to encourage and give the proper credit to a faithful God who has lovingly guided my life. Credit is given to my husband also, whom I love dearly. He trained himself to serve others in dentistry and heard God's call himself and answered at the right time.

"The One who calls you is Faithful. He will do it" (1 Thess. 5:24, NIV).

# About the Author

arol Spurgeon has degrees from Southwest Baptist University in Bolivar, Missouri and Southwest Missouri University in Springfield Missouri. She considers her life as a wife, mother, grandmother, homemaker, self-taught artist, writer and volunteer of most note. She was born in Strafford Missouri but lives in Great Falls, Montana. Serving the church of her youth as well as the Body of Christ now, these surprising extraordinary accounts are sure to inspire, appreciate and encourage the "How Could He's" of any ordinary life.

CPSIA information can be obtained
at www.ICGtesting.com
Printed in the USA
FSOW04n1758101117
40841FS